Twayne's New Critical Introductions
to Shakespeare

MACBETH

Michael Long

*Lecturer in English, Cambridge University
and Fellow of Churchill College, Cambridge*

TWAYNE PUBLISHERS · BOSTON
A Division of G. K. Hall & Co.

Published in the United States by Twayne Publishers
A Division of G. K. Hall & Co.
70 Lincoln Street
Boston, Massachusetts 02111

Published simultaneously in Great Britian by
Harvester Wheatsheaf
66 Wood Lane End, Hemel Hempstead, Herts.

Twayne's New Critical Introductions to Shakespeare, no. 9

Library of Congress Cataloging-in-Publication Data

Long, Michael, 1941–
  Macbeth/Michael Long.
      p.   cm. — (Twayne's new critical introductions to
Shakespeare)
  Bibliography: p,.
  Includes index.
  1. Shakespeare, William, 1564–1616. Macbeth.   I. Title.
  II. Series.
PR2823.L65   1989
822.3′3—dc20   89–15567
ISBN 0–8057–8720–8.   CIP
ISBN 0–8057–8721–6 (pbk.)

To Laurette

Titles in the Series

General Editor's Preface

The *New Critical Introductions to Shakespeare* series will include studies of all Shakespeare's plays, together with two volumes on the non-dramatic verse, and is designed to offer a challenge to all students of Shakespeare.

Each volume will be brief enough to read in an evening, but long enough to avoid those constraints which are inevitable in articles and short essays. Each contributor will develop a sustained critical reading of the play in question, which addresses those difficulties and critical disagreements which each play has generated.

Different plays present different problems, different challenges and excitements. In isolating these, each volume will present a preliminary survey of the play's stage history and critical reception. The volumes then provide a more extended discussion of these matters in the main text, and of matters relating to genre, textual problems and the use of source material, or to historical and theoretical issues. But here, rather than setting a row of dragons at the gate, we have assumed that 'background' should figure only as it emerges into a critical foreground; part of the critical endeavour is to establish, and sift, those issues which seem most pressing.

So, for example, when Shakespeare determined that *his* Othello and Desdemona should have no time to live together, or that Cordelia dies while Hermione survives,

his deliberate departures from his source material have a
critical significance which is often blurred, when discussed
in the context of lengthily detailed surveys of 'the sources'.
Alternatively, plays like *The Merchant of Venice* or
Measure for Measure show Shakespeare welding together
different 'stories' from quite different sources, so that
their relation to each other becomes a matter for critical
debate. And Shakespeare's dramatic practice poses different
critical questions when we ask – or if we ask: few do –
why particular characters in a poetic drama speak only in
verse or only in prose; or when we try to engage with
those recent, dauntingly specialised and controversial
textual studies which set out to establish the evidence for
authorial revisions or joint authorship. We all read *King
Lear* and *Macbeth*, but we are not all textual critics; nor
are textual critics always able to show where their
arguments have critical consequences which concern us
all.

Just as we are not all textual critics, we are not all
linguists, cultural anthropologists, psychoanalysts or New
Historicists. The diversity of contemporary approaches to
Shakespeare is unprecedented, enriching, bewildering.
One aim of this series is to represent what is illuminating
in this diversity. As the hastiest glance through the list of
contributors will confirm, the series does not attempt to
're-read' Shakespeare by placing an ideological grid over
the text and reporting on whatever shows through. Nor
would the series' contributors always agree with each
other's arguments, or premises; but each has been invited
to develop a sustained critical argument which will also
provide its own critical and historical context – by taking
account of those issues which have perplexed or divided
audiences, readers, and critics past and present.

Graham Bradshaw

Contents

Preface

This book is about one of the greatest dramas in the world. No two people see or read it alike, so nobody need expect to agree with everything I have written here. My aim is not absurdly to lay down the critical law but to aid and instigate. Some of the aid is straightforward, where I say what I feel scene by scene so that a fellow student of *Macbeth* may run his or her thoughts against mine in dialogue. Some of the instigations by contrast are less straightforward, especially when I take off from the play on comparative excursions designed to send the enthusiast in quest of other dramatic and literary works to which, in my scheme of things, *Macbeth* relates.

The most straightforward section is Chapter Four. It works through *Macbeth* scene by scene, with emphasis on the unfolding rhythm and shape of the work as we watch it on the stage or try to visualise it in the mind's eye. Perhaps it should have come at the beginning, but I have chosen instead to broach some more general issues before settling down to a sequential analysis. A reader of course may prefer to ignore my decision and tackle the most straightforward section first.

The least straightforward section is the latter part of Chapter Two. Here I hazard some wide-ranging comparisons of *Macbeth* with other literary and dramatic works, both more ancient and more modern than Shakespeare's drama. I have ventured these comparisons in the conviction that a great work of art is an inspirer of enthusiasm. The richness of a work like *Macbeth* makes one want to linger on every last syllable of it; but it also sends one off in all sorts of directions, inspired by its force and magnitude to seek out other things which it calls up in the imagination as its fellows. I hope the fellows I have found for it will not look like instrusive strangers to other people.

The remaining three chapters come between these two extremes. Chapters One and Three stick to *Macbeth* for the most part, but instead of working through it as it unfolds they aim to make general observations about some of the principal verbal and visual images which bring the play as a whole to life. Here too I have tried to stress the theatrical nature of the work, since plays are plays and even as we read them we should still be trying to see them on a stage. Chapter Five sets *Macbeth* in relation to some other plays. Most are by Shakespeare. Some are tragedies by other dramatists.

This emphasis on theatre has also caused me to refer from time to time to Verdi's operatic version of *Macbeth*. It is the least successful of his three Shakespeare operas but is still a highly stageworthy version of the original. It has its splendid as well as its rather ludicrous moments, provides a good foil for the play, and is as thought-provoking as any work of critical interpretation.

ACKNOWLEDGEMENTS

I have used many editions of *Macbeth*, from the First Folio onwards, and have learnt a great deal from many of its modern editors. Quotations in this book come from what is still the best single volume edition of his works, that of Peter Alexander (Collins, 1951).

My greatest debt is, as always, to my wife, not least in the case of this book because her theatrical imagination is quicker and better trained than mine.

The Stage History

The devotee of dramatic production in the late 1980s has been able to see *Macbeth* in all manner of guises. During the last year alone, the play has been splendidly and classically produced at Stratford and rather less classically produced in a fringe version which makes Malcolm something like the villain of the piece. Both Chinese and Japanese productions, each much closer to the original than the vivacious fringe travesty, have played in Britain during the same period, and Verdi's modulation of the play into the medium of opera has been further modulated into the fast-growing medium of the opera film. It has been a busy twelve months.

All this effervescence dates back four hundred years to the late 1580s, when Raphael Holinshed brought out his *Chronicles of England, Scotland, and Ireland*. Holinshed was not much of a historian by our standards, but he was a fine teller of tales, with a strong, dramatic turn of phrase when it came to curdling the Elizabethan blood with accounts of wickedness and treachery. In one of his stories of eleventh-century Scotland, he told of the 'inward malice' against his own king which a soldier called Donwald felt 'boiling in his blood' and how, 'kindled in wrath by the words of his wife', he broke into the king's chamber 'a little before cock's crow' and killed him, the 'abominable murder' being followed by 'monstrous sights'

such as horses eating their own flesh and an owl strangling
a hawk; and in another story from the same period he
sent further shivers up the Elizabethan spine by telling
how King Duncan, 'soft and gentle of nature', was killed
by Macbeth, another man egged on by a fierce wife
('burning in unquenchable desire to bear the name of a
queen') and further undone by 'three weird sisters' who
accosted him 'in strange and wild apparel, resembling
creatures of elder world'.

   This is rousing stuff, already half-way to the stage, and
one of those roused was Shakespeare. A generation after
the lively *Chronicles* appeared, Shakespeare, who had
already plundered Holinshed to great effect for his history
plays, went back to his old favourite and plundered him
again. He ran together the two stories about king-killers
driven on by evil women to give us *Macbeth*. Holinshed
deserves his place in the great play's history for the high
melodrama of his prose style and the vivid psychology of
his two portraits of black-hearted traitors. Shakespeare's
play, wonderful in psychology and unafraid of melodrama,
owes more to him than just its plot.

   It may well be that *Macbeth* was written for performance
at court. Its royalism is strong and such things as witches
who can fly and '*vanish*' seem perhaps to call for a stage
with 'machines', beyond the range of the popular, outdoor
theatre. It has elaborate, masque-like spectacles too, as
when its eloquent stream of apparitions rises from the
witches' cauldron. King James, first monarch of the newly
united England and Scotland, supposed descendant of
Banquo, a stickler for the Divine Right of Kings, an
expert on witches and a liker of plays which were not too
long, is an obvious candidate for the attentions of the
author of *Macbeth*. A performance at Hampton Court
may well have occurred, but if it did we know nothing
about it.

   We do know about a performance in the popular theatre
in the spring of 1611 when Dr Simon Forman, an
astrologist, went to the Globe and took notes. He recorded

having seen witches, Duncan's court, the killing of the king, prodigies, the flight of the princes, the murder of Banquo, Banquo's ghost, the killing of Macduff's family, the sleepwalking of Lady Macbeth, the liberating army from England and Macduff's killing of Macbeth. This makes it clear that something resembling the play we now have was seen in the ordinary playhouse. It would have been played in broad daylight, with Shakespeare's poetry being quite enough (as indeed it obviously is) to conjure up the play's gruesome world of the night without benefit of the actual darkness and intermittent torches which an indoor, court performance could have provided.

After Shakespeare's death, *Macbeth* suffered the common fate of his plays—revision, for gentlemanly taste. Sustained dignity was required, less knotty verse, and more overt moral meanings. Music and spectacle were wanted too, for 'divertissement' as Pepys put it in 1667 with regard to Sir William Davenant's version of *Macbeth* which kept real Shakespeare off the polite stage from the 1660s until the middle of the eighteenth century. The play became a statuesque kind of 'opera' (baroque opera being the high form of drama in this period). Elegance and constant elevation were the keynotes, making for something rather grand, but much less terrifying than what Shakespeare, and indeed Holinshed, had provided.

Thereafter, as with many other plays, the theatre story involves the rescue of the uncouth Shakespeare from the hands of his tasteful improvers. All the great names of the eighteenth- and nineteenth-century theatre are involved. In the mid-eighteenth century Garrick got rid of most of Davenant (though adding some improving stuff of his own), and a generation later Kemble and Mrs Siddons sought to explore the compelling psychology of Shakespeare's two protagonists, though we must wonder how far they could have done so given the persistence of the statuesque acting style.

Then came Edmund Kean. It is with Kean that we sense the power of Romanticism's recovery of Shake-

spearian depths and terrors, unmodulated into the polite
and classical. It is Kean above all whose Shakespearian
performances we would want to be able to recover, to
see how the greatest actor of the age of Coleridge and
Hazlitt put on the stage what they put into their essays
and annotations. Hazlitt, on *Macbeth*, talks of 'the
wildness of the imagination and the rapidity of the action',
and Kean was the actor who seems best to have caught
this 'wildness' and 'rapidity' and thus taken people nearer
to Shakespeare than they had been for nearly two centuries.

Throughout the nineteenth century the theatre, like
criticism, explored the possibilities which Romanticism
had unearthed. Macready in the mid-century and Irving
a generation later explored the depths and complexities of
the play's psychological life, trying to get inside the fears
and fragilities of the hero and evoking the fierce forces in
life which drove him helplessly along. The depths and
contradictions of the driven mind were the compelling
things. Heroic greatness was also pitiful littleness. Coleridge's Macbeth, terrified of the 'phantoms of [his] own
brain' and racked by 'the affliction of the terrible dreams',
set the tone for the nineteenth-century theatre.

Shakespeare and Holinshed would surely have approved,
just as they would very likely have approved of Verdi's
attempt, at the same time and inspired by the same
motives, to get the spirit of Shakespeare into the musical
idiom of Italian Romanticism. Verdi is Shakespeare's
champion in the opera ('I have had his works in my hands
since my early youth. I read and reread him constantly').

But there was a price to be paid for all this. The
powerful and admirable Romantic tradition tended to give
more and more of the play to the Macbeths, and often to
Lady Macbeth more than to her husband (Verdi's opera
should really be called *Lady Macbeth*), and while people
were gripped by Shakespeare's tremendous account of the
dark night of their souls the rest of the play receded. Back
in the eighteenth century Samuel Johnson had still thought
of the Macbeths in a more public way, as the murderous

creators of misery for others and not only as sufferers themselves, and he had finally dismissed them from the centre of his stage: 'Lady Macbeth is merely detested; and though the courage of Macbeth deserves some esteem, yet every reader rejoices at his fall.' But Romanticism tended to lose that dimension. Shakespeare's play has the Romantics' suffering protagonists in it, but it also has a public dimension, alive in the strong decencies of its 'minor' characters, in its magnificent symbolism, and in a radiant verse which overflows with a sense of human goodness caught in familial, natural, religious, soldierly and cere-monial images.

In the twentieth century, criticism has often tried to restore this dimension but production has by no means always followed. One strand of modern theatre production has indeed further accentuated the partiality of the Romantic response, giving Macbeth all the play's life and turning out contemptible opponents for him. The fringe production already mentioned is an example of this, as was Polanski's awful film. Both 'improve' Shakespeare's text, as Davenant did, but now with the different aim of draining the play of its heroic aspects and making the minor characters so mean in scale that the Macbeths, of course, tower over them. There is something absurdly easy and sentimental about the process, as there was in Davenant.

But that is not the whole story. Many productions have not succumbed to the easy option of belittling, nor to any other kind of simplifying concentration on the protagonists alone. The Stratford version mentioned above was one such, poignantly evoking the deep satisfactions of family, kin and kind from which the Macbeths were dreadfully excluded, every bit as much as it evoked the dreadful exclusion itself. It is impossible to summarise the rich and varied story of *Macbeth* in twentieth-century performance (let alone its fascinating modulation into such things as Kurosawa's *Throne of Blood* or Ionesco's *Macbett*), but I hope it is more than personal prejudice which makes me think that the best of the twentieth-century theatre has tried, however hard it may be, to bring alive both halves of the play. I think Shakespeare's bias lay that way too, as did that of the humble Holinshed who wanted to stir up his readers with tales of 'inward malice' and 'unquenchable desire' but also to appal them, by showing the havoc that such things make in the wider human community where other people are 'soft and gentle of nature'.

The Critical Reception

It is easier to be a critic of a play than actually to put it on the stage. This may be enough to account for the fact, as I see it, that twentieth-century criticism has more often kept in touch with both halves of the play than has the theatre. As we move from the nineteenth to the twentieth century in *Macbeth* studies, there is a big change. The great protagonists still get the attention they deserve, but the world of the other characters now also comes back into prominence, as does the symbolism which makes that world.

Two classic essays, preceded by a classic book, catch this moment of transition. The book is Caroline Spurgeon's, concentrating on Shakespeare's imagery, and the essays are those of L. C. Knights and Cleanth Brooks. All three are less theatrical than they should be, all three smell of the study rather than the stage; but they mark a point of divergence both from Romanticism and from theatrical realism. They put the poetic images back, and not only those which belong to the Macbeths. This makes them seminal. They teach us how to win back the other half of the play.

Behind them is G. Wilson Knight, our century's most exuberant imaginer of Shakespeare's verbal and theatrical images of blackness and the light. It takes no great smartness to catch him out being wild. But he has done more for Shakespeare in critical print than any other twentieth-century author. The other half of *Macbeth* benefits from his lyrical and indefatigable attention to 'life themes'.

After these four, others have consolidated the work on the play's other half. Christian critics have been to the fore in stressing its sacred ceremonial of goodness; but Shakespeare, like Wilson Knight, is an unsafe eclectic in religious matters and though this play has its madonna and child (Lady Macduff and her son) and ends with 'Grace', its religion is not only Christian but also Hebraic (its verse teems with the seeds of *Genesis*) and pagan (it ends with the green boughs of fertility carried by young warriors undergoing initiation). Such factors are apt to make the Christian critics sound more like special pleaders than restorers of balance.

Something of the same applies to readers who have got back the other half by relating the play to the Renaissance court and its festal masques. This has its point, but no masque ever made Birnam Wood move or the seeds of nature stir like the chthonic *Macbeth*. Court masques are a-glitter with the power-consciousness, easy philosophy and conspicuous consumption of their aristocratic participants. *Macbeth* is rough stuff by comparison, and incomparably deeper stuff as a result.

Better justice is done to both halves of the play by writers about tragedy who ask how it is that the criminal sinners are both justly and unjustly dispatched from the world of the good. What sort of a world-picture do we need to contain them? How can we divide our loyalties and our perceptions of ourselves subtly enough neither to sentimentalise nor to abuse their stature? Tragedy has provided better answers to this than Christianity, aided by the tragic philosophers of the nineteenth century, Schopenhauer and Nietzsche, and their ideological descendants in modern psychological tradition, notably Jung. Jung's idea of the conscious mind and its unconscious 'shadow' is arguably the best place to start looking for a critical–ideological equivalent of *Macbeth*'s vision of the destructive but necessary dark.

Then there is feminism. Feminism is one of the liveliest presences in modern criticism and Shakespeare is standing up to its enquiries very well. There may not yet be a great feminist book on Shakespeare but there will be before long. If the student of *Macbeth* is a woman, and even more if he is a man, feminist criticism will be vital. Whether or not they are 'better' than other critiques, the books in the bibliography whose titles proclaim this sort of interest take, at this moment, a special precedence.

This is also true of writings by oriental scholars. As in the theatre so in the study, some aspects of Shakespeare have come easier to minds formed outside the Western tradition, and Japanese and Indian readers in particular have shown themselves well placed to understand the forms, shapes and rhythms of Shakespeare's theatre. Several oriental theatres taught Peter Brook how to stage Shakespeare unforgettably. How much is there still to come from non-European critical sources?

Marvin Rosenberg has to be mentioned. More a filing cabinet than a book, in dimensions as in nature, his work on *Macbeth* contains 802 pages. Most of it is scene-by-scene analysis, where his mind is usefully eclectic. But it also contains long lists of stage performances and adaptations in several languages and countries. It is a mine of useful information.

New readers embarking on all this would do best (a) to give no critic too much authority, (b) to be ready to venture outside literary criticism and (c) to think about other tragedies too. They should also (d) be ready to read other plays by Shakespeare which are not tragedies but which contain, as *Macbeth* does, ceremonials, initiations, collapses of individual identity and green boughs. These plays are called comedies. Many critics have used them well in exploring the structure and significance of *Macbeth*. Northrop Frye and C. L. Barber are their patrons.

· 1 ·

A Brief Play in a Unique Medium

THE FOLIO TEXT

Macbeth was published for the first time in 1623 when, seven years after Shakespeare's death, John Heminge and Henry Condell brought out a collected edition (the First Folio) of their former colleague's works. Half of the plays in this momentous volume had already appeared in one or more Quartos, printed as single plays with or without the permission of their author or his company. *Macbeth* however was one of those which had never been printed before, so this text of 1623 is our sole authority.

The Folio text presents its difficulties, but *Macbeth* was relatively well printed and its problems are by no means as numerous or as intractable as those of some other plays. The signs are that it was printed from a theatre prompt-book so that, with its many stage directions and its careful designation of who speaks what, it would seem to represent what actually appeared on the Jacobean stage. This does not make it definitive, since plays written for performance are fluid, easily altered things. Parts of it may be missing, cut from the performance of which our text seems to give us a record; or material may have been added, not necessarily by Shakespeare. All in all it is a relatively clean text, and an excellently theatrical one; but since it is the only text, there can be no appeal from it to anything else when we suspect that something may be wrong.

The consensus has come to be that Hecate is probably an addition to Shakespeare's original, but there is no certain proof of this. Even if she is an addition it may well be that Shakespeare would not have objected to her. She is worked in well enough and scarcely does any harm to the play on stage. Beyond that there are a series of unresolved worries, widely or less widely shared.

Two recurrent problems with a bearing on production and critical opinion are the drunken porter in II.iii and the testing of Macduff by Malcolm in IV.iii. The porter has been thought by some to be beneath Shakespeare's dignity and probably therefore an addition. He has been found duller than the normal run of Shakespeare's vigorous 'low-life' characters, and he has sometimes been felt to be out of key either with the idiom of the play in general, which contains little of such humour, or with the awesome tenor of the local context in which he appears. Malcolm's testing of Macduff has also been found problematic, not because its point cannot be explained (for it shows what happens when political tyrannies make unguarded words dangerous) but because that point is less oddly made elsewhere and because, once again, the idiom and pace of the passage differ from the play's norm.

Another question of this kind concerns the evocation, also in IV.iii, of the pious English king with his heaven-blest powers of 'healing benediction'. This has occasionally been felt obsequiously to flatter James I and thus, even in a play with exceptionally strong royalist leanings, to be rather extraneous. Its poetry is so fine as to worry few people, but it does occasionally crop up as a minor stumbling block, as if it were the relic of a royal performance of the work rather than an integral part of the play which Shakespeare 'really' wrote.

Such falterings, or alleged falterings, in the idiom and rhythms of the play have worried actors and directors. Editors have also had to fret at little inconsistencies and wrinkles in the text which it would take a very shrewd spectator to notice at all. Two scenes in which off-stage events are recounted present such problems. The first is I.ii, where the wounded Sergeant reports on the various battles and rebellions which precede the play's action and where impossible muddlings of different things have sometimes been found and adduced as evidence of textual corruption. The second is III.vi where Lennox discourses with a Scottish Lord about events which, it would seem, have not yet taken place, suggesting to many that the scene should come later.

There is also an oddity concerning the sons of Duncan. It is possible to wonder whether they aren't bundled out of the play a little briskly after the murder of their father, and whether Donalbain might not have merited a mention, if not a second appearance, when his elder brother assumed the crown. This too has suggested incompleteness to some anxious scanners of the Folio text.

Some of these things have worried editors trying to prepare an authoritative text, others have nagged at actors, directors and readers trying to pick up the movement of the work and feeling some snag or catch in it at these points. A Quarto, even a bad one, might sometimes have helped, though the chances are that it would have made us pay for its help by posing yet further questions. But all there is in the end is this single text, happily rather a good one, together with a mass of bibliographical, editorial, theatrical and critical response to it.

THE BREVITY OF MACBETH

But by far the most curious and striking thing about the text of *Macbeth* has nothing to do with these controversial passages. The really odd thing is that it is so short. At about 2,100 lines, *Macbeth* is one of the shortest plays in the Shakespearian canon and by far the shortest of the great tragedies. *Hamlet, Othello, King Lear, Antony and*

Cleopatra and *Coriolanus* are all more than half as long again. Far more peculiar than Hecate, the porter, the vanishing princes, flattery of James I or any of the textual inconsistencies or irregularities of the Folio text is this extraordinary brevity. It is the key to the uniqueness of *Macbeth*, to how the play feels, and to how it asks to be directed.

In his comedies Shakespeare is sometimes brief, though seldom as brief as this. But in the tragedies and historical dramas he is a maker of complex plays with many people in them where plenty of time is given to secondary stories and minor characters. The plays are long because his poetic world is various and thickly peopled. It is in the nature of *Hamlet*'s world to be crowded, to have no single centre, and to surround and baulk its hero with endless, baffling complications. It is in the nature of *King Lear* to be gigantic and all-encompassing, so as almost to overwhelm its audience and make them feel the strain involved in rising imaginatively to its stupendous vision. It is in the nature of *Antony and Cleopatra* to meander and linger idly, dispersing tension and taking time to look at a wide world beyond the central pair.

But it is in the nature of *Macbeth* to be swift and utterly single-minded. For once Shakespeare is uninterestd in subplots and very little interested in his customary comic admixture to the tragic tone. To get the single, sweeping thing he wants he is prepared, in the second half of the play, not only to abandon a minor figure like Donalbain but to limit even so great a figure as Lady Macbeth to a single scene. Readers and spectators of this marvellously compact, powerful play have regularly been struck by the fierce pace it generates from the first instant. Coleridge expresses what everyone feels when he notes how it sets off at high pitch, without *Hamlet*'s 'gradual ascent from the simplest forms of conversation to the language of impassioned intellect', and so does Bradley when, following Coleridge, he describes the play's beginning as one in which 'the action bursts into wild life' and when he judges

Macbeth to be 'the most vehement' and 'the most concentrated' of the tragedies.

SHAKESPEARE'S POPULOUS STAGES

It was in fact an audacious experiment on Shakespeare's part to give up on this occasion the big scale of the other plays. He was giving up not some accidental and unimportant feature of his drama, but something close to the heart of it. The big, eventful, populous spread of his historical and tragic stage is an index of the breadth of his human vision. His decision to forgo such a thing in the case of *Macbeth* was, we do well to realise, very bold.

In the other, lengthy dramas Shakespeare's representation of the human world is of unequalled richness. His harmonies are composed from more voices than are those of other dramatists, and shot through with more dissonances. His human stories are told with an abundance of details and particulars, and his plays contain a wealth of such stories enacted simultaneously. The world he sees is of infinite variety, and he surpasses all other writers in the ability to paint it. He creates a wider range of human beings than any other writer, and catches all their different voices with endless dramatic resource.

His tragic stage is thus not made only for heroes and his historical stage is not made only for kings. Secondary characters usually get a good hearing in the Babel of his theatre. Some of them manage to make themselves immortal with only a couple of scenes in which to do it; and some succeed, with hardly more than a well-placed phrase or two inserted into some big, group scene to make us remember, however inconveniently, that the world is not all harmony, let alone unison. There are times when his kings and heroes are almost rudely jostled from the centre of attention. Their affairs, however huge in import they may think them to be, regularly have to make way for somebody's private complaint or for some obstinate individual opinion. If the world is such that, as Hamlet says, 'a king may go a progress through the guts of a beggar', then the stage that paints the world will have to present beggars and their guts as much as kings and their progresses. Shakespeare's well-peopled stage does this better than any other.

He gives evidence of this wonderful breadth throughout the canon. The comedies, whose world is smaller and more intimate than that of the histories, none the less feature many characters who trouble the dominant romance strain profoundly. His romance writing is of the very greatest lyrical beauty, but its speakers still have to rub shoulders with all sorts of bystanders, not all of them necessarily impressed by romance beauties; and in the history plays, his eye and ear for the teeming variety of the world's people were hard at work from the beginning of his career.

Already in the first group of history plays, dealing with the reigns of Henry VI and Richard III, he portrays a huge world stretching from the north of Britain to the South of France where diverse people compete for our attention. Then in the second group, especially in the great double play of *Henry IV* at the heart of it, he lets us hear speakers from every region and every social class of Britain, finding different voices for them all and crowding them together in a giant play with no itch to shape everything into a single, convenient meaning. *Henry IV* is the crowning achievement of his work in the chronicle play, and one of the supreme masterpieces of his theatre. It is a monument to Shakespeare's humanism, which consists in just this abundance, this unreadiness to overlook any individual life in the interests of some grand design or simplistic historical theory.

This prodigality in the creation of diverse human beings continues in most of the tragic plays. Complex worlds are depicted in *Hamlet, Othello, Coriolanus* and *Antony and Cleopatra*. Lives other than those of the tragic heroes are given with full dramatic empathy, and some of the people who live alongside the tragic protagonists move us as much as the heroes themselves. If we pay attention to what happens to Ophelia, Desdemona, Menenius and Enobarbus in the four tragedies listed above, we shall see how unready Shakespeare is to give his stage uniquely to his heroes. Our involvement with these secondary characters is intense. 'Some innocents', says Cleopatra, 'scape not the thunderbolt', and the crowded kind of drama which Shakespeare normally writes is ideally equipped to record that fact.

The author of these four plays is a master sociologist, fascinated by the dynamics of social groups as well as by the individuals who dominate them. He is a close observer of all the ways of being Danish, Venetian, Roman, or Egyptian. Cast-lists are long, sub-plots abound, and anyone may, at any moment, seize the dramatic initiative to make us see the world for a while through his or her eyes. The heroes breathe the same air as common citizens and common soldiers. There are no special, privileged realms allotted to the tragic great ones, no kinds of enquiry to which they may not be exposed and no levels of language, high or low, excluded from their world.

AUERBACH AND JOHNSON

In his great book *Mimesis*, a monumental study of the different ways European literature has found to admit the ordinary world into high, and especially tragic, literature, Eric Auerbach defines this Shakespearian quality very well. Shakespeare, for Auerbach, exemplifies the 'Hellenic' as opposed to the 'Hebraic' strain in European literature, and the 'creatural' as opposed to the 'figural' strain in Christian tradition. His world is composed from Hellenic colour and concrete detail and from the flesh-and-blood, creatural this-worldliness with which some kinds of Christianity leaven a religious–allegorical or figural view of the world. His tradition is represented in the ancient world more by Homer than by the Old Testament, and in the medieval world by the Franciscan spirit of creatural solidarity.

Hence it is that Shakespeare's plays portray a world which is 'agitated' and 'multilayered', full of 'the great variety of phenomena'; hence his concern with 'the concrete portrayal of the everyday processes of life', with 'rendering the most varied phenomena of life', and with 'the manifold conditions of human life'; hence his theatre's 'rich scale of stylistic levels'; and hence of course his predilection for mixing tones, 'the sublime and the low, the tragic and the comic'.

Such a vision of Shakespeare reveals very well why his stage is normally full of diverse people. It reveals why the plays have to be long and complex. His Hellenic and creatural humanism requires rich, novelistic detail in story and character. He needs room to let everyone speak and be noticed; and he needs to mix the tragic with the comic in order faithfully to represent what Samuel Johnson, another eloquent devotee of this tonal mixture and another celebrant of Shakespeare's populous world, calls 'the real state of sublunary nature', with its 'chaos of mingled purposes and casualties'. These plays, for Johnson, catch this 'chaos' better than the writings of lesser authors, and the key to their doing so is that characteristically Shakespearian mixing of tones which creates what Johnson calls 'the mingled drama':

Shakespeare's plays are not in the rigorous and critical sense either tragedies or comedies, but compositions of a distinct kind; exhibiting the real state of sublunary nature, which partakes of good and evil, joy and sorrow, mingled with endless variety of proportion and innumerable modes of combination; and expressing the course of the world, in which the loss of one is the gain of another; in which, at the same time, the reveller is hasting to his wine, and the mourner burying his friend; in which the malignity of one is sometimes defeated by the frolick of another; and many mischiefs and many benefits are done and hindered without design.

The comic part of the 'mingled drama' is by no means confined to particular scenes or reserved for particular characters. It is in the grain of the plays throughout. It constantly counterpoints the high tone of tragedy with an awareness of the indignities and commonplaces of life. The absurd, the petty, the unbecoming and the 'frolick' coexist, 'without design', with the high passions, great crimes, heroic sufferings and terrible 'malignity' of tragedy. Big plays are required for the theatrical representation of how 'the high and the low co-operate in the general system by unavoidable concatenation'.

KING LEAR: SATURNALIA AND THE GROTESQUE

King Lear, the fifth of these huge tragedies, is in many respects different. Archetypal or primordial images, roles and locales replace, in some senses, the specifics of 'sublunary nature' found in the other plays. King, master, servant, father, daughter and son appear in large part as timeless, symbolic roles, freighted more with legend, folklore and myth than with the accidents of 'unavoidable concatenation', while the locales of palace, house and heath have a similar universality. Composed of such primary, undifferentiated things, *King Lear* in some senses turns away from the mingled 'chaos' of the other plays, and the world it reflects is less 'without design'.

However, other factors combine to give it its own version of Auerbach's Hellenism and Johnson's 'mingled purposes and casualties'. Like the other plays, *King Lear* is shot through with comedy. Its terrors and grandeurs coexist throughout with the chatter of the Fool, the Foolish King, and the mock-Fool Edgar, so that few of its images of pain and suffering, however awesome and sublime, can quite shake off the accompanying sense of the absurd and the undignified. Such considerations inspire two classic studies of the play, in which Wilson Knight discusses its 'comedy of the grotesque' and Enid Welsford relates its tragic imagery to the comic upset of Saturnalia and the 'sottie', or grotesque pageant of fools.

Further, *King Lear* has a sub-plot, that classic feature of the crowded stage. Shakespeare's greatest tragic hero is obliged to share his stage with another man and the most elaborate of all his secondary stories. The story of Gloucester and his sons often parallels the story of Lear and his daughters, but equally often it is quite different, as if unwilling simply to provide obedient parallels for the main events. The two overlapping but different stories share the play and concede space to each other, and for this too scale is of the essence.

But the brief, swift, patterned *Macbeth* audaciously abandons all this. It gives its hero more exclusive attention than do the other plays. It has no sub-plot. It contents itself with comparatively slender characterisation of its tapestry of secondary figures. It has hardly any comedy, to such an extent that many people have found it an awkward intrusion when the porter tries to introduce what might have been ordinary comic currency in the other plays. It is full of imagery which is, in Auerbach's terms, more 'figural' than 'creatural', and it concentrates on undifferentiated, archetypal images more exclusively than *King Lear* and quite differently from any of the other plays. The world it paints is by no means 'without design'.

It stakes its life not upon a complex and large-scale representation of what Johnson called 'the course of the world' but upon the intensity, symbolic simplicity and naked, radiant clarity of its high and often sacred images. Revellers do not hasten to their wine while mourners are burying their friends. Creatural detail is limited, as is stylistic range. Instead of Shakespeare's familiar world with its 'chaos of mingled purposes', it gives us a high-intensity, single-focus world of conspicuous shapeliness.

Its imagery, verbal and visual, is extremely patterned. It lives more exclusively than any other Shakespearian tragedy on such simple, basic dualisms as day and night, summer and winter, brightness and murk. As it lingers in our minds after repeated performances and readings, we can recall its entire life to ourselves by thinking of such elemental polarities as are represented by (say) cherubim and witches, the saint and the criminal, the martlet and the crow, or the green boughs of spring and the 'sere' of the dying world. It gives the impression of having been conceived whole, in a single instant, and it lives on in the mind as an instantaneous thing, as much a visionary pattern of light and dark as a story unfolding in time. It was thus very hospitable to two famous studies, by L.C. Knights and Cleanth Brooks, which sought to elevate imagery above story and pattern above character in Shakespearian drama. *Macbeth* made their work much easier than any other tragedy would have done.

Its concentrated power is often the power of the sacred, the pagan-sacred as well as the Christian-sacred. Sacred images abound. We have the feast, the table and the cauldron; the sword and the dagger; the forest, the castle, the bed, the tomb; childbirth, murder and sacrifice; wounds and blood; armour and royal robes; old men with white beards and young men 'in their first of manhood'. It often seems to have less in common with other Shakespearian plays than it has with highly symbolic works, like the songs of Blake or *The Rime of the Ancient Mariner*, where we have rare, uncluttered access to the naked essentials of things.

This tragedy therefore does not need, for once, the long cast-list, the sub-plots and the numerous clashing or interwoven stories. It does not need to be long. It needs, as Coleridge put it, 'the invocation. . . made at once to the imagination'. It needs, as Bradley said, to be 'tremendous'. It goes straight to the core of primal conflicts without impediment, undeflected by irony and uncluttered by too much detail, and the passionate ritual of its non-realist theatre draws images from legend and myth to sustain its 'tremendous' pitch and its sense of the fate of the tribe.

Such a play, in varied adaptations, makes a fine Japanese samurai film. It takes well to African and Oriental stages. It tempts Verdi to turn it into a heroic, national opera, and Strauss to make it into the most heroic of his tone poems, both looking for the right idiom even if neither is quite successful. On the other hand, its grandeur dies in realist modes, as in Leskov's story of *A Village Lady Macbeth*, or in productions which try to mute its flamboyant voice. *Macbeth*, said Luschino Visconti, 'is opera'.

It is at any rate sacred drama, a symbolic play about primary things. But to be such a play successfully, it must substitute for the loss of creatural abundance a compensating richness of symbolic life. Its images must be wrought to great intensity if the abandonment of a wide world of human detail is not to result in something more limited than Shakespeare's other tragedies.

Two of the play's most striking means for achieving this are the visual theatre, including the theatre of symbolic locales, and a peculiar resort to soliloquy and other forms of solo speech. Both are extremely developed in *Macbeth*, making its dramatic medium radically different from that of the other plays. They give *Macbeth* its special feel and special intensity.

THREE PROPS

As centrepieces to its visual theatre, *Macbeth* contains three of Shakespeare's greatest props. The first is the feasting table, in III.iv. It speaks of hospitality and largesse, of the ceremonial of order and degree, of the

trust and security of a well-lit, indoor world, safe from
the darkness and danger of the night outside. The Scottish
Lord of III.vi provides a good commentary on it when
he longs for the return of what it represents, so that:

>   we may again
> Give to our tables meat, sleep to our nights,
> Free from our feasts and banquets bloody knives,
> Do faithful homage and receive free honours –
> All which we pine for now;
>
> (III.vi.33–7)

but it is characteristic of *Macbeth* that we should have
not only this commentary but also a visual representation
set before us on stage.

The second, the mighty opposite of that, is the cauldron
of IV.i. While music ushers the guests to the feasting
table, chanting and incantation introduce the horrible
cauldron. Nature here is torn into fragments. Bits and
scraps are tumbled pell-mell together in a hideous cookery
whose 'gruel thick and slab' is an antitype to the food of
'feasts and banquets', symbolising the nauseous violation
of things 'even till destruction sicken'.

The third is Birnam wood, with its symbolism of the
returning spring. Youth, sap and growth are evoked by
the sacred–magical advance of the forest's 'leavy screens'.
The scene has no connection with the military manœuvres
of the history plays or the soldiering of Rome, where
armour is made of metal and leather, not of the forest's
boughs. The origins of this great image are in the comedies,
where forests and leaves are regularly treated as deep and
saving sources of renewal. Here as there, young people
who have had contact with what Northrop Frye calls
Shakespeare's 'green world' emerge from the experience
to repossess a human house fallen into sickness.

No other Shakespearian tragedy depends so much on
such set pieces of visual theatre. The non-linguistic
resources of *Macbeth* have a uniquely major role in
the play's realisation. Action and meaning are visually

elaborated throughout, from the 'fog and filthy air' of its highly charged beginning to the returning light and clarity of its ceremonial end.

FOUR APPARITIONS

In keeping with this stress on the visual is the play's series of apparitions, making in their turn for a powerful theatre of mime. There are plenty of ghosts in Shakespeare, and a number of dumb shows, but *Macbeth* is unique in the degree of its reliance on such things, and certainly in the dramatic intensity to which it repeatedly lifts them.

The witches themselves are the play's first apparitions, beings as yet unknown and unnamed who swirl out of the mist and storm at the beginning and are able, according to the stage direction in their next scene, not just to exit but to '*vanish*'. Only *A Midsummer Night's Dream* and *The Tempest* give so large a role to the supernatural as the witches introduce into *Macbeth*.

Then there is the air-borne dagger at the beginning of Act II, which may be real, and thus 'sensible to feeling', or may be a 'dagger of the mind'. It lives like the witches on some fearful boundary between the real and the imagined, where clear forms blur and the 'heat-oppressed brain' is horrified to see the patterns of its imaginative world dissolving into the shapeless unknown.

Then there is the ghost of Banquo, living on the same boundary, visible to Macbeth but invisible to others and thus inducing some of the same mental perplexities as the dagger. It has, as Hamlet's father's ghost has on its second appearance when only Hamlet can see it, deep psychological suggestiveness, as well as appalling spiritual truths to utter by the silent presence of its 'gory locks' and blank eyes.

Finally there are the apparitions conjured from the cauldron, which could have been mere melodrama in lesser hands. But they are bound in with the play at large by their participation in its series of mimes and by their thematic continuity with the rest of the work. They too are real and unreal, and they can drive Macbeth to distraction by their partial eloquence, simultaneously revealing and withholding what he wants to know.

These are the play's four main apparitions; but they are set off and intensified still further by the general background of sights and portents seen or imagined. An aura of supernatural terror attaches to almost everything, and the theatre of visions, spectres and nocturnal visitations contributes greatly to the play's uniquely 'tremendous' effect.

THREE SETTINGS

In keeping with this stress on visual theatre, the settings of the play's scenes are also very important. Location and terrain are never accidental matters in *Macbeth*. All sorts of opportunities are given for production to make setting and locale into living features of significant design. Chief among them are the three different human dwellings where the three main phases of Macbeth's life are enacted.

First there is the domestic setting of his own house at Inverness, with its atmosphere of hospitality and family life. People are feasted and given lodgings for the night in what, until criminality and terror take hold of it, is a 'pleasant seat' where the summer air is sweet and the martlet comes to breed, as much a 'guest' of the place as Duncan and his train.

Then, after the king's murder and Macbeth's seizure of power, comes the royal palace. This is a bigger, grander, more formal place, the setting for the ritual feast and for Macbeth's doomed attempt to live out the great images of kingship. The Folio gives no stage direction to tell us that Act III has moved to the palace at Forres, but editors are right to want to insist on it and directors right to follow them. This is not the domestic 'pleasant seat' in the country, but the great centre of power which the usurper has seized.

Then finally, when the masquerade of kingship has collapsed and Macbeth rules by naked power alone, there is the castle of Dunsinane whose fortifications he feverishly secures and extends:

> Great Dunsinane he strongly fortifies.
> Some say he's mad; others, that lesser hate him,
> Do call it valiant fury.
>
> (V.ii.12–14)

It is the bleak setting for his final solitude. All companionship has deserted him. His tormented, suicidal wife keeps to an inner room, with a pitiful candle by her bedside. After the pleasant house at Inverness and the great palace at Forres, the castle of Dunsinane is Macbeth's bunker.

One does not quite want to say that house, palace and castle are symbols, for they are also made of wood and stone. But they do have peculiar eloquence as dramatic locales, marking out with grand simplicity the main stations of Macbeth's life. They contrast powerfully with each other; and they also combine together, as varieties of human habitation, all set against the foggy wilderness outside, the leafy forest and whatever sort of den it is that the witches inhabit.

SIX THRESHOLDS

If places are so significantly different from one another, it follows that transitions from place to place will be momentous. *Macbeth* is in many ways a play of thresholds, involving rites of passage and initiations. Its concept of space is sacred, its world given shape and meaning by significant demarcations.

In the other plays, space is normally a simple fact of 'sublunary' life. People walk the rooms and corridors of Elsinore and the streets of Venice and Cyprus without necessarily passing through momentous transitions in their lives as they go. The same is true of the streets and houses of *Coriolanus'* Rome, and of the vast Mediterranean and near-Eastern world over which *Antony and Cleopatra* wanders. These plays deal for the most part in secular geography. There are special moments when great thresholds are crossed, often involving a passage from indoors to outdoors. Thus Coriolanus is bundled and jeered out of the gates of Rome, Ophelia's body carried out of Elsinore to the graveyard, Lear driven out into the storm with the gates barred and bolted behind him. But such moments of significant transition are special, while in *Macbeth* they are the ordinary currency of the drama. Apart from the movements from Inverness to Forres and Forres to Dunsinane, there are at least six major thresholds crossed in the play. Six times someone goes through a doorway and the step changes everything.

The first occurs when Duncan arrives at Macbeth's house. To pass beneath Lady Macbeth's battlements, croaked in by a hoarse raven, is to make a 'fatal entrance' into a new world. It is not just to go through a gateway, but to cross a threshold of destiny. Shakespeare stresses this momentous entry, making us visualise the battlements with the gateway far beneath where the horses pass through. We seem to look down on the scene with the eye of the raven whose ugly voice describes the nature of the threshold crossed.

A similar step is taken when Macbeth enters the 'pit of Acheron' to revisit the witches. Here too a door is involved:

Open, locks, whoever knocks,

(IV.i.46)

and this too is a 'fatal entrance' into a new world, as Macbeth underlines by speaking of initiation as he plans the visit:

My strange and self-abuse
Is the initiate fear that wants hard use.

We are yet but young in deed.

(III.iv.142–4)

He will be very much older in deed once he has taken this step, hardened and transformed through overcoming an 'initiate fear'.

His step into the witches' den leads to another step involving another significant doorway, through which Macbeth bursts by proxy when his hired killers break in upon the domestic privacy of Macduff's home. They intrude upon mother and child like violators of a sanctuary. Males invade a female space, adults a child's space, armed men a domestic space. They bring knives into a haven of non-violence left fatally unprotected.

The killing of Macduff's family is Macbeth's final atrocity, but it has all followed logically and inexorably on from the 'fatal entrance' he made when he committed his first crime, for he passed through his most momentous doorway when he went into the chamber of the sleeping king. It was a horrible mission of intrusion, fraught with the idea of setting sacrilegious foot in a holy place. To intrude thus, and then to pass on into the innermost sanctum, bursting in through the curtain of the king's bed and thrusting a dagger in through the skin of his 'unguarded' body, is to make nothing less than 'a breach in nature/For ruin's wasteful entrance'. It is the step of all steps, the violation of all violations, irredeemably initiating Macbeth into evil and misery.

But these four doors through which men step into nearer contact with evil and death are balanced by two more doors which open, so to say, in the opposite direction. The first is the door opened by the porter and made awesome by that insistent knocking. De Quincey, in his famous essay about the knocking, said that 'it makes known audibly that the reaction has commenced; the human has made its reflux upon the fiendish; the pulses of life are beginning to beat again'; and Verdi seems to have felt something similar, echoing in his opera the retributional knocking and entrance of the Commendatore in Mozart's *Don Giovanni* by giving his Banquo some noble, Commendatore-like lines to sing as he enters. The effect should not be exaggerated, but there is a perceptible 'reflux upon the fiendish' as this door opens to let in the early light of dawn.

But the true 'reflux' comes, of course, when Malcolm's army comes to Dunsinane and recaptures the kingdom. Here again the sense of initiation is very strong, as young, beardless, 'unrough youths', serving in the army of 'the boy Malcolm', are blooded in their first battle, with all the air of spring ritual which their green boughs suggest. The 'powers above' have 'put on their instruments' to give events their sense of inevitability. Resistance is minimal, Macbeth is 'ripe for shaking' like some autumnal fruit whose time has come, and the castle is 'gently rendered' to them like some precious gift or reward. There is magic in the process, culminating in the moment when the victorious young liberator is formally invited to step through the play's last doorway: 'enter, sir, the castle'.

FOUR CHAMBERS

But though Inverness, Forres, Dunsinane and the witches' den are important settings, the most wonderful locales in the play are four which are never visited. There are two bedchambers in *Macbeth,* made incomparably vivid to the mind's eye even though we never enter them, and two sealed cells briefly but unforgettably evoked in the verse. In the two bedchambers terrible disruptions occur, shattering sleep and everything that sleep stands for, while in the two sealed cells creatures lie in uninterrupted repose. These four chambers, balanced and linked in imagery, do as much as anything seen on stage to chart the play's symbolic, spacial world.

The first of the bedchambers is Duncan's. We may have to pinch ourselves to remember that we have never actually seen the bed, the old man, the blood on the sheets and on his 'silver skin', and the drugged grooms smeared with gore. Two overwhelming recollections of it by Lady Macbeth imprint it indelibly on the memory. The scene in the chamber before the murder is evoked by her paralysing, childlike perception of the sleeping king:

> Had he not resembled
> My father as he slept, I had done't;
>
> (II.ii.12–13)

and the scene afterwards is called up much later, in what Bradley finds 'the most horrible lines in the whole tragedy', when she remembers going back into the room and being for a second time transfixed: 'who would have thought the old man to have had so much blood in him?'. Writing could hardly do more to awaken our sense of the atmosphere and significance of a place, helped of course by the play's continuous stress upon locale, and by that fateful doorway, visible or sensed in the dark, which leads from the empty, fear-ridden stage of II.ii to the little, trusting group of sleepers lying 'within'.

The second bedchamber is Lady Macbeth's, about which the Doctor of Physic and the Waiting-Gentlewoman converse at the beginning of Act V. While in his sacred chamber Duncan slept the sleep of the just, 'shut up in measureless content', free from suspicion or fear, and accompanied by his trusted grooms, Lady Macbeth, in her sick-room, long tormented and undermined by

> the affliction of these terrible dreams
> That shake us nightly,
>
> (III.ii.18–19)

goes in lonely fear of the dark. Her heart is 'sorely charg'd' and her mind 'infected'. This bedchamber and sick-room, where she 'has light by her continually', is a vivid microcosm of 'perturbation', contrasting with Duncan's chamber which was a microcosm of peace, tranquillity and innocence. Dreadful violence is done to the human body in one of these rooms and equally dreadful violence suffered by the mind in the other. Sleep is murdered in both.

The vividness of the mental pictures conjured up by these private rooms is such that two further chambers where creatures lie, each mentioned only briefly, join them in the play's design, haunting the mind in their turn as if they had been set on the stage. The first is the nest of the martlets, the delicious 'pendent bed' and 'procreant cradle' of their breeding, hanging high up in the summer air; and the second, under the quiet ground, is the royal tomb at Colmekill, the 'sacred storehouse' of the remains of Duncan's ancestors and 'guardian of their bones'. Beautiful, innocent, sanctified lives, uncontaminated by the horrors of Macbeth's world, begin in the one and end in the other, lapped in each case in a close-sealed chamber. The martlets' nest is the play's richest symbol of unviolated content and quiet growth, focusing in a simple, natural symbol all the play's beautiful sense of the breathing, breeding life which Macbeth simply cannot destroy; and when Duncan lies with his fellow kings in a tomb which is called a 'storehouse', the place seems replete with garnered riches in no way cut off by death. These two places relate to what was once the undisturbed bedroom of a reposeful king, and they contrast with grim rooms where terrible dreams are visited upon unquiet sleepers to 'shake us nightly'.

SOLO SPEECH

Such a drama of vivid locales and visual effects is extremely charged and economical, helping to make *Macbeth's* brevity potent rather than schematic; and it is matched by a verbal feature of the play which also helps to keep up its high pitch. This is solo speech, in which dramatic dialogue gives way to soliloquies, asides, confessions, conjurations and lonely cries. *Macbeth* thrives on the

peculiar intensity and unmediated quality of speech
uttered in solitude and outside the exchanges of normal
communication.

The abundance of solo speech is one of the reasons
why the ambiguities of humour are as foreign to this play
as they are native to other Shakespearian tragedies, and
why, in consequence, the porter's unique intrusion of
humour is often found irksome. The solitary voice plunges
down to the depths of the soul to bring up whatever it
finds there. It brings hidden, private thoughts straight to
the surface, confessing them to the speaker's self, revealing
them to the skies or to the overhearing audience. This is
a stark business done in black and white, without the
lights, shades, and iridescences of humour.

There are many different kinds of solitary speech in the
play, all conspiring to put enormous strain on actors.
Some are extended and evident. Some are brief, fleeting
things. Some are monosyllabic. Some are brooding, some
furious. Some are terrifyingly sudden outbursts. Some are
delivered on a stage where the speaker is alone, some are
asides uttered when a preoccupied speaker turns away
from others to look inwards. Some are reported, as this
or that character recalls sounds and cries that he or she
has overheard, directed to no particular auditor. The
device is so rich and curious, again giving *Macbeth* its
unique dramatic medium, that it is worth detailing in full.

SOLO SPEECH–ACT I

In Act I Macbeth has two full-blown soliloquies. First he
broods on the witches' 'supernatural soliciting' in scene
iii; and then he begins scene vii with:

If it were done when 'tis done, then 'twere well
It were done quickly.

(I.vii.1–2)

The second of these is a pure, Hamlet-like piece of self-interrogation, but the first contains more than one kind of self-directed or non-directed speech, for the true soliloquy is only a part of a sequence of fractured asides whispered by Macbeth when the witches take possession of him and he is 'rapt'. Interpersonal discourse fractures like this throughout the play, sometimes forming into long, self-addressed set pieces, sometimes breaking down into brief cries and mere noises in the void.

The range of solo speech types in this first act is already extensive. Macbeth turns away from Duncan's court at the end of scene iv to utter what is partly an aside, addressed to himself, and partly an invocation to the 'stars' to 'hide [their] fires'; and this, the first of the play's many invocations, is followed in the next scene by the biggest and most famous of them, when Lady Macbeth conjures 'spirits/That tend on mortal thoughts' and bids them 'unsex' her.

Invocation is the dominant mode of her solitary speech but it is not the only one. It is preceded by speech which she, alone on stage, addresses to the absent Macbeth and by the reading of the letter in which Macbeth's thoughts are spoken aloud in the voice of his wife. Both are modes of utterance which disrupt the normal line connecting speaker to auditor, giving words the intense, haunting quality of free-floating sound, emanating from the mouth of one creature but never to arrive at the ear of another.

SOLO SPEECH–ACT II

In Act II the trend continues, with one full-blown soliloquy and a host of other types of solo speech. Again the full-blown soliloquy, in scene i, turns out really to contain two distinct forms of discourse. In the second part of it Macbeth addresses himself in the classic manner, but in the first part he speaks to the 'fatal vision' of the dagger. Two different kinds of heightened effect are involved, each as haunting as the other.

In the second scene numerous types of solo speech are deployed. Lady Macbeth talks to herself on stage alone; then Macbeth cries out alone off-stage; then she talks to herself again. Macbeth then enters, and ordinary interpersonal discourse between them begins; but no sooner has it begun than Macbeth is quoting the cries of half-awakened sleepers calling out 'murder!' or 'amen!', and telling how he heard the sound of someone who 'did laugh in's sleep'. And then he quotes in horror the solitary cry of that tremendous 'voice' which called out, perhaps to him, perhaps to 'all the house', perhaps just into the night: 'sleep no more!/Macbeth does murder sleep. . .'.

It is an extraordinary series of effects, making one start edgily at every sound, hearing repeated cries in the dark. But there is more, for the scene goes on to include a brief passage of classic soliloquy in which Macbeth thinks of his bloodstained hand reddening the 'multitudinous seas', and it ends with him addressing the unknown, off-stage intruder whose dreadful knocking at the door is heard in the scene's closing lines:

Wake Duncan with thy knocking! I would thou
could'st!
(II.ii.74)

Furthermore, we hear mention of 'the owl-scream' and 'the cricket's cry'. These are mere sub-verbal, animal soliloquies; but by the time we have watched this great scene and listened to the variety of its fractured sounds we may well be far from clear about where human voices stop and animal cries begin.

We go on hearing noises in scene iii. The porter's mumbling is soliloquy in its way; but the scene's most memorable solo speakers are those evoked by Lennox, talking of the events of the 'unruly' night with what sounds like a catalogue of the varieties of solitary utterance. He reports 'lamentings heard i' the air', 'strange screams of death', and 'prophesying, with accents terrible'. The 'obscure bird' has 'clamoured the livelong night'. In such an atmosphere, even the bell which rings at the end may begin to sound vocal and organic like the rest of them, and it is possible to find oneself wondering whether the knocking at the gate was really done by Macduff and Lennox or whether that too might not have come from some creature of the night expressing itself in solitary tattoo.

SOLO SPEECH–ACT III

III.i begins and ends with conventional kinds of solo speaking. Banquo starts it like a narrator keeping us up with events:

Thou hast it now–King, Cawdor, Glamis, all
As the weird women promis'd

(III.i.1–2)

and Macbeth ends it with a rhyming couplet of formal closure. This closing couplet is purely conventional, but Banquo's introductory narration strays into more personal accents as he broods on what the witches have promised, adding meditative interiority to his formal lines of introduction.

In between we hear Macbeth brood in full-blown soliloquy about how his fears 'in Banquo/Stick deep'; and we also hear his catalogue of dogs, which is more likely spoken to himself, in private exorcism of his self-disgust, than offered to the murderers by way of canine information. It is indeed often acted as some kind of semi-aside, as if in recognition of the fact that the tendency to turn away from the interchanges of discourse to brood in solitude is now endemic to the play.

In scene ii there are four lines of confession from Lady Macbeth, in which she reveals to herself, as she would not have done to her husband, how the fruits of their crime are enjoyed 'without content'; there are more night-sounds, such as Hecate's 'summons' and the 'drowsy hums' of the 'shard-borne beetle'; and there is another conjuration, addressed by Macbeth to the 'seeling night' as he once again turns aside from his interlocutor to speak out into empty space.

Then, after the murder of Banquo in scene iii, where there are disembodied if not solitary voices in the dark, there is the banquet. Four times in this scene Macbeth turns aside from his fellows to speak alone about 'saucy doubts and fears', about dead men who rise again to 'push us from our stools', about blood which 'will have blood', and finally about having 'strange things' in his head 'that will to hand'; and four times likewise he speaks to Banquo's ghost, which his bewildered guests perceive as speaking into nothingness.

By the time Act III ends with the wary Lennox speaking to the Old Man with as much indirection as possible, steering clear thereby of dangerously open verbal contact, it would seem that semi-directed, undirected, or otherwise solitary speech has virtually become the play's norm. As if to underline that fact, Lennox utters to the skies a conjuration no more particularly addressed than to 'some holy angel', hoping that such a being may be there to obey his hopeful injunction that it 'fly to the court of England'.

SOLO SPEECH–ACT IV

The witches' incantation at the beginning of Act IV, addressed with one voice to themselves as a collective entity, extends still further the play's range of self-addressed speech forms. There are also more background cries uttered by a cat, a hedgehog, and 'Harpier'; and then there are the four responses of Macbeth to the witches' apparitions, sounding in part like contributions to a formal ritual and in part like bemused, fretful soliloquy. In the latter part of the scene, when the witches have vanished, Macbeth introduces the new solo speech form of the curse, anathematising 'this pernicious hour', and then turns aside from personal exchange once more when he tells himself (rather than Lennox) that nothing shall henceforth come between his 'thoughts' and his 'acts'.

The act closes with the most sustained piece of interpersonal dialogue in the play, spoken in England by Macduff, Malcolm, and Ross. Such speech sounds a distinctive note in a play where people do not normally talk to each other for so long. But even here background cries in the void are heard. There are 'sighs', 'groans' and 'shrieks' rending the air of Scotland; and there is another speaking bell, 'the dead man's knell', adding its inanimate voice to the lamentations of the earth's creatures.

SOLO SPEECH–ACT V

The opening of Act V brings in yet another kind of solitary speaking. What Lady Macbeth says in her sleep assumes the form of a long, fragmented soliloquy; but talking while asleep is soliloquy of yet another distinct type, where the mind's guards and mechanisms of repression are shockingly removed and the speaker is at the mercy of her ungoverned tongue. She speaks to herself and quotes to herself a scrap of rhyme. She speaks to her absent husband, and perhaps quotes some of his words. She repeats things once spoken by herself in dialogue, but they have now drifted away from their addressee and seem almost to have come loose from their source in her own being as well. She speaks involuntarily to the whole listening world of the audience, making uneasy eavesdroppers of us all as she voices such things as are normally not voiced at all, or else discharged only in secret to 'deaf pillows'. The communicative functions of speech are violated more completely in this scene than anywhere else, and the fabric of interpersonal discourse presented in extreme and pitiable disarray.

As the play moves from here to its close Macbeth speaks almost entirely to himself. He has two full-blown soliloquies of despair, on 'the sere, the yellow leaf' and on the 'brief candle' of a life 'signifying nothing', and a third fragment of such soliloquy when he admits to being 'aweary of the sun'. He also utters fleeting asides and confessions about forgetting 'the taste of fears' and doubting 'the equivocation of the fiend'; and he has simpler self-assessments to voice in formulation of his own condition, such as when he finds himself 'bear-like' at the stake or declares himself unready to 'play the Roman fool'. These closing scenes are like a long soliloquy from him, spoken on and on through all the comings and goings of the action, as his soul slowly dies and he watches it die.

Even so he does not have a monopoly of solitary utterance. We hear the play's last cry when Lady Macbeth's death is greeted by 'the cry of women', and there is a complex, solo performance on stage from Macduff, speaking to the absent Macbeth, to the audience, to himself, to his sword and to 'fortune', before going off to find his man and avenge his country's misery and his family's annihilation.

SOLITUDE AND BONDING

There is nothing like this in any other Shakespearian play. Such continuous self-communing, self-interrogation and confession are unknown elsewhere. They help give the play its brevity and its constant high pitch by collapsing the discursive details of daily speech. People are always apt to speak from awesome inner depths, addressing themselves nakedly to matters of truth and falsehood, good and evil, salvation and damnation, with very little deflection or dilution of such immense concerns. Their hopes, doubts and terrors rise unimpeded to the surface in a way that happens less in plays which, though they are busy with such things, are also busy with the social networks of everyday utterance.

But perhaps the deepest role of solo speech in *Macbeth* is to suggest, as part of the bedrock of the play's vision, a primitive, largely nocturnal loneliness in creatural life, conveyed by the cries both of animals and of men and witnessed to by all sorts of lonely talking. There is a side to the play which captures and reveres the daylight bonds of loyalty, 'concord' and 'human kindness', from which are made the court, the clan, the kingdom and the whole structure of all 'humane statute'. Voices linked here in kinship and security are of rare and beautiful radiance. But there is another side to it, perceived when people speak alone, where the concord breaks and primitive insecurity reigns. Separate voices crying in the night speak of a deep, contrasting solitude in creatural life, set over against the bonds of kin and constantly intruding on the life of the bonded group or the socialised human being. The play's very medium thus embodies a vision of primal solitude in constant competition with bonding, the one dark, brooding and violent, the other clear, bright and gentle. The drama shows how the two coexist in human life, how they come and go in the soul like night and day.

· 2 ·

Doers of Deeds

BLOODY EXECUTION

Shakespeare often begins a tragedy with somebody's description of the protagonist before he comes on stage. We hear of Marcius as 'chief enemy to the people' before he bursts in full of fury. We hear of the 'good and gracious' Timon before he sweeps on distributing largesse. We hear of Antony falling into 'dotage' and then the great lover strolls on in leisured magnificence. We hear whispers of Lear's odd shifts of favour and then he comes on in state to express his 'darker purpose'. And we are told that Othello is a vainglorious soldier full of 'bombast circumstance', as well as a lascivious, black lover who has stolen a white women, before the man himself appears as if to answer these nasty charges. The simple technique creates expectation. It also tells an audience whom to watch, and why.

Macbeth's introduction comes from the wounded Sergeant in I.ii. The Sergeant is a fine, epic soldier with a bent for vivid rhetoric, and the picture he paints is memorable. He evokes the rebel Macdonwald with the 'multiplying villanies of nature' swarming on him like flies on a carcase surrounded by an equally swarming horde of 'kerns and gallowglasses' drummed up for his cause in the Western Isles, and then he describes the tremendous irruption of

Macbeth into these swirls of movement, cutting his way
to the centre of things to dominate them with his deeds
and his presence:

> brave Macbeth – well he deserves that name –
> Disdaining fortune, with his brandish'd steel
> Which smok'd with bloody execution,
> Like valour's minion, carv'd out his passage
> Till he fac'd the slave;
> Which ne'er shook hands, nor bade farewell to him,
> Till he unseam'd him from the nave to th' chaps,
> And fix'd his head upon our battlements.
>
> (I.ii. 16–23)

This 'bloody execution' sounds brutal; but the epic rhetoric
also makes it sound magnificent.
The Macbeth we later meet does not disappoint the
expectations raised by this dramatic opening account of
him. He is brutal, but he has his epic magnificence too,
and one of his chief roles is to be the sort of decisive
doer, intervener or irruptive agent whom the Sergeant
describes. The Sergeant makes us think about violent
action, but also about action in itself, as he pictures
Macbeth's terrible, thrilling intervention into things and
his ruthless domination of the field. This will be a play
about a man who does, and about the momentous deed
that he does. It will be a play about doing, and about
that spectacular, frightening spirit of 'bloody execution'.
Macbeth cannot lie passive like Duncan 'shut up in
measureless content', nor stand like Banquo 'in the great
hand of God', waiting patiently for the unravelling of
destiny. They may live in tranquillity at the slow pace of
unfolding events, as the martlets do, suspended in their
airy bed where 'the heaven's breath/Smells wooingly', but
the restless Macbeth must be up and doing. Early on he
hopes that chance may crown him, 'without my stir', but
he soon realises that it will not. He must stir, and act,
and thus confront the fatality of individual deeds.
Shakespeare makes this sense of the existential fatality

of action resonate powerfully in the play, and his principal method for doing so is extraordinarily simple. *Macbeth* activates every possible resonance of the verb 'to do'. 'Do', 'did', 'done', and the cognate noun 'deed', are words stirred into vivid life by an imagination dwelling profoundly on the fatal business of 'bloody execution', or indeed any kind of execution. They carry the play's cogent exploration of what it is to be a separate, acting individual rather than an unperturbed particle of social acquiescence or of the breath of nature's quiet.

They are aided in this by another word, almost as simple, and allied both conceptually and onomatopoeically with 'do' and 'deed'. This is the verb 'to dare', upon which the play also dwells to wonderful effect. Macbeth does. Macbeth dares to do. These simple words are made to yield every gram of their poetic and philosophical potential.

ACT I: 'IF IT WERE DONE WHEN 'TIS DONE'

In I.iii Macbeth entertains his hope that things might happen 'without my stir'. But in the next scene Duncan names Malcolm as his heir, Macbeth's fond hopes die, and his imagination turns to the mechanisms whereby desires become deeds. He will have to stir, to 'o'erleap' the obstacle in his path, and he will have to act, hidden guiltily from the lights of the natural world:

> Stars, hide your fires;
> Let not light see my black and deep desires.
>
> (I.iv. 50–1)

Banquo and the king stand before him talking pleasurably and easefully. They are still in the old, quiet world, but Macbeth has moved to another realm. This is the start of his career as an existential agent, and the start of the formidable poetic career of the verb 'to do':

let that be
Which the eye fears, when it is done, to see.

(I.iv. 52–3)

In the next scene, when his wife receives his letter and
the witches' poison starts to course through her veins, the
keywords sound again in juggling conjuration:

Thou'dst have, great Glamis, that which cries
'Thus thou must do' if thou have it;
And that which rather thou dost fear to do
Than wishest should be undone.

(I.v. 19–22)

Lady Macbeth conceives of herself as a natural doer, made
for 'business' and 'dispatch', but we shall see how the
stresses of the interventionist role will be too much for
her. Macbeth's greater trepidation is well placed. It is
more appropriate to the terrors attendant upon the business
of doing, and to the explosive powers which lie within
these fascinating words.

In the last scene of Act I the keywords come thick and
fast. Macbeth wrestles with his fears and desires, and the
keywords flicker hypnotically before his captivated eyes:

If it were done when 'tis done, then 'twere well
It were done quickly.

(I.vii. 1–2)

They draw him on with the idea of decisive, 'be-all and
end-all' action. Then comes a counter-movement, equally
strong, where he remembers the great taboos which speak
'against the deed' and shrinks in anticipation of the outrage
which will be felt when 'the horrid deed' is revealed.

Then his wife chides him for his doubter's sense of 'I
dare not', and he seizes on that word too and squeezes it
tightly:

I dare do all that may become a man;
Who dares do more is none.

(I.vii. 46–7)

The word 'man' has joined the wrestling knot of words, and Lady Macbeth keeps it there to shame him into action:

> When you durst do it, then you were a man.
>
> (I.vii. 49)

By the end of the scene Macbeth is resolved, and a dark, subdued hymn to doing sounds beneath the couple's dialogue. Lady Macbeth talks horribly of an outrageous licence to do what one will:

> What cannot you and I perform upon
> Th' unguarded Duncan?
>
> (I.vii. 69–70)

Macbeth hits on the clever idea of incriminating the grooms so that people will think 'they have don't', and Lady Macbeth chimes excitedly back that there will be none who 'dares receive it other'. They chant together, work up their courage, and bring Macbeth to readiness for 'this terrible feat'.

ACT II: 'I HAVE DONE THE DEED'

As Act II opens, the incantations stop while Banquo evokes the magically profound 'pleasure' and 'content' of Duncan's soul, but after this beautiful linguistic interlude the phantom dagger appears. It lures on the 'heat-oppressed brain' of Macbeth, rekindles 'the heat of deeds' and renews the fatal drive to action: 'I go, and it is done.'

In II.ii the awesome words are whispered in terror in the dark. Lady Macbeth fears the attempt has been bungled ('tis not done'), and dwells on the awful irony whereby they might be confounded not by doing 'the deed' but by failing to do it. She too is now more alert to the scale of what is involved, increasing the weight on the key verb by using it in another momentous context:

>   Had he not resembled
> My father as he slept, I had done't.
> (II.ii. 12–13)

By the time the crime is accomplished, the collocation of verb and noun is enough to sound the depths of irrevocability: 'I have done the deed.'

The now appalling noun 'deed(s)' shudders in their minds three more times in the scene ('these deeds', 'this deed', 'my deed'); and in the midst of them Macbeth finds another memorable collocation, linking doing with daring in an expression of the utmost horror:

> I am afraid to think what I have done;
> Look on't again I dare not.
> (II.ii. 51–2)

Such simple words will never be simple again.

After this great scene Shakespeare lets the words go for a while, before bringing them back to close the act. In II.iv, with the Old Man's talk of 'the deed that's done', Ross's reference to 'this more than bloody deed' and Macduff's mention simply of 'the deed', we hear uneasy speakers probe the keywords suspiciously. They keep what has happened at arm's length by referring to it darkly as 'the deed', as if they wanted to keep their eyes averted from some abomination or their persons out of striking distance of it.

The atmosphere of their talk makes Macbeth's deed of destruction seem like the deed of Adam and Eve. All nature has fallen into darkness and savagery as a result of it. Macduff already knows that Ross will not see things 'well done' at Macbeth's coronation. From such catastrophe recovery cannot be so quick, for Macbeth has made 'a breach in nature' with his tremendous intervention into the settled state of things, and these three are now living amidst the 'ruin' which, as in Eden, gained its 'wasteful entrance' when that breach was made.

ACT III: 'A DEED OF DREADFUL NOTE'

But deeds lead to deeds and in Act III the words return, with the Second Murderer 'reckless what I do' and Macbeth determined that his new deed, the killing of Banquo, 'must be done tonight'. In III.ii Lady Macbeth tries to kill the words off with the finality of her statement that 'what's done is done', but it will be a long time yet before the terrible energy of these words has run down. Macbeth, better apprised than his wife of the enormity of what they have unloosed, promises to keep up with the race of things:

> there shall be done
> A deed of dreadful note,
>
> (III.ii. 43–4)

while his bewildered wife asks him 'what's to be done?'; but he, as if sensing her inability to stay the course on which they are now set, decides to keep his doings to himself:

> Be innocent of the knowledge, dearest chuck,
> Till thou applaud the deed.
>
> (III.ii. 45–6)

There is now a hardening in Macbeth. The fateful words no longer frighten him so much. He begins to use them with perceptible relish, sensing their menace and less awed than he was. That 'dearest chuck' is gross and sinister in a way that is new; and also new are some tellingly banal uses of the keywords in the next two scenes. In III.iii the murderers banalise the words with shop-talk about 'what we have to do' and the report they will deliver on 'how much is done', and in III.iv there is a thuggery in their professional talk of cutting throats ('that I did for him'). Macbeth seems to catch this thuggish note from them like a contagion, hoping that they not only cut Banquo's throat but also 'did the like' for Fleance, and calling one of them a 'nonpareil' among men 'if thou didst it'. At some level he seems to be enjoying this new brashness, as if it were man's talk for which his 'dearest chuck' is unfitted.

But he loses his swagger when the ghost appears to shake his 'gory locks' at him. The keywords are now used to cry helplessly 'which of you have done this?' and to disavow the role of agent altogether: 'thou can'st not say I did it.' To fight back this terror he will need the talismanic verb 'to dare'. He will need to claim that he

> dare look on that
Which might appal the devil

(III.iv. 58–9)

and to face down the charge of cowardice with cries of 'what man dare, I dare' and 'dare me to the desert'. These are cries that come swirling out of a mind in panic, until at last he regains some shreds of composure, enabling him to return to things that 'must be acted', and to the accent of menace: 'we are yet but young in deed'.

ACT IV: 'A DEED WITHOUT A NAME'

To make himself less 'young in deed' in Act IV he returns to the witches, who were the original inspiration for the impluse to do. As he sets foot in their den he cries out with the verb: 'what is't you do?', and they chant back the noun as if in ritual response: 'a deed without a name'.

While Duncan's court lived at the pace of acquiescence and unassertiveness, this den is the holy place of a religion of deeds. It is where Macbeth goes for inspiration when his heart 'throbs to know' and when, unable to wait upon the quiet rhythms of nature's evolutions, he is prepared to see

> the treasure
Of nature's germens tumble all together,
Even till destruction sicken

(IV.i. 58–60)

to satisfy his restless desire. He gets his inspiration. He
emerges from the ordeal nerved again, resolved to kill for
a third time and with the keywords on his lips:

> The flighty purpose never is o'ertook
> Unless the deed go with it. . .

(IV.i. 145–6)

>   And even now,
> To crown my thoughts with acts, be it thought and
>   done. . .

(IV.i. 148–9)

>   No boasting like a fool:
> This deed I'll do.

(IV.i. 153–4)

ACT V: 'LITTLE IS TO DO'

The deed he does is the killing of Macduff's wife and
children, and after it Shakespeare leaves the idea of doing
alone, as if, after such an outrage, it could now have no
further moral or poetic content. The remainder of
Macbeth's life is led in Act V within the fortress of
Dunsinane, where, incapable of any more doing, he paces
out the long, halting soliloquy of his despair, interspersed
with outbursts of rage against puny people like servants,
unwilling followers, a messenger and 'the boy Malcolm'.
It is the nadir of the great doer, hemmed in and frustrated
in every desire.

Here, as his way of life falls into the sere, there is no
further activation of 'do' and 'deed', and the idea of daring
takes on a desperate, last-ditch quality. He is tied to the
stake, with only growls of defiance as evidence of his
former courage and nerve. We have seen enough of deeds
and doers. Doing has turned out merely to be butchery
and the compelling rhythms of the keywords have run
down.

As the rhythms of doing fade, a different rhythm, not felt since Duncan was alive, brings time round in its cycle again to make the autumnal Macbeth 'ripe for shaking'. His fall does not feel like an act performed by men, attributable to human agency. It happens when the time is ripe, in accordance with some internal logic in events which is not subject to will and intervention. We wait until the long night of his deed-filled tyranny at last 'finds the day' and then we find the fortified castle being 'gently rendered' to beautifully unurgent men.

In harmony with the ease and gentleness of that phrase come two magnificent usages of the keywords which help slow the play to a less cruel pace. The first comes from Macduff, who has no quarrel with anybody except Macbeth and who, rather than fight against men innocently embroiled in the tyrant's career, would prefer to leave his sword 'undeeded'. The second comes from Old Siward, inviting Malcolm simply to walk into the castle of Dunsinane, crossing its threshold effortlessly since, miraculously, 'little is to do'. The tenor of these phrases is relievingly unassertive, as if what were occurring involved no more than acquiescence in the eternal cycles of things.

The human world comes back into contact with an inner, pre–conscious rhythm. Green branches bring the forest's silence and fertility back into human society and the young king promises that 'what's more to do' will, as if in response to the forest's presence, be 'planted newly with the time'. Things will be done according to the old, quiet rhythm of things, 'in measure, time, and place', with no doing, daring, 'bloody execution' or 'dispatch' disrupting the free-flowing 'grace of Grace'. We have not heard such sustained sounds of leisure and peace since Duncan was alive, or since Macbeth started to conjure the turbulent life out of dangerous words, or since the witches wound up the infernal plot with that frantic cry which has proved to be so laden with import:

I'll do, I'll do, and I'll do.

(I.iii.10)

PRIMORDIAL CRIMINALS

In one realm *Macbeth*, deploying these keywords, shows us a great, criminal deed and then a chain of consequential deeds, each as horrible as the last and all leading to destruction. To that extent it contains a simple but extremely powerful moral vision according to which Macbeth is a damned and self-damned creature, 'black Macbeth' as Malcolm calls him, the 'butcher' with a 'fiendlike queen' at whose fall, in Johnson's words, 'every reader rejoices'.

But there is another realm to the play, and another effect produced by its concentration on doing and daring. In this realm the keywords make us think not of these particular deeds but of deeds and doing in general, and here there is something about Macbeth which is beyond the range of the judgmental certitude expressed alike by Malcolm and Dr Johnson. In this metaphysically complex part of the play there is something fatal, doomed, but heroic about Macbeth, and something which makes him not the disruptive outsider of whom the world is well rid but the representative outsider, the outsider such as we all are, the archetypal representative of the fact that, as conscious, acting individuals, not trees of the forest, we cannot simply stand 'in the hand of the great God' but are fated to be involved in deeds.

In this respect the play echoes the Christian myth of the Fall. Macbeth and his wife re-enact the deed of Adam and his wife, and they also embody some aspects of Satan. There is a sacred play in *Macbeth*, dealing with the primal fact of doing and the primal offence of being a doer. But, as is often the way with attempts to tell the Christian story of the Fall, the apparent moral does not entirely survive the story's telling. The images of the story are apt to speak for themselves, and not always to the same effect as the moral, so that tales of Satan, Adam and Eve in revolt against God tend to be knotty. We are apt to see inalienable aspects of ourselves in these original sinners, and their fate represents to us tragic things about an imperfect world rather than simple, revelatory things about disobedience. We take to some extent the criminals' part, so that Malcolm's simple words are not quite enough to sum up what we feel about their careers.

In this sacred play of the primordial crime the hero's deeds are not only criminal. The doer, with his interventionist audacity, is a much more widely representative man, gifted and cursed with the human attributes of agency and consciousness. He has courage, individual consciousness, and will-power, and in his inability to acquiesce patiently in the primal order of things we sense a strong, restless energy which is compelling. He is still a terrifying criminal who spreads death and destruction about him. But there are aspects of his being to which we respond because, for better or for worse, they seem intrinsic to the business of being human. In the disturbing, tragic figure of the primordial criminal there is something which draws our empathy, something which Wilbur Sanders, in his powerful, Nietzschean reading of the play, calls a 'compelling energy of defiance'. This elevates him above butchery, and takes him metaphysically out of range of simple verdicts.

MILTON'S SATAN

This is why Milton's Satan, creator of the first breach in the Christian cosmos, owes so much to Macbeth. Milton once considered tackling Macbeth as a dramatic subject, and in a sense he did tackle it when he created the Satan of *Paradise Lost*. For Milton's Satan shares with Macbeth the paradoxical mixture of criminality and greatness, and this mixture makes them complex and difficult in similar ways. They both exhibit heroic nerve and unnerved despair. They both seem full of power and, almost at the same time, quite powerless. They can seem huge and menacing or pitifully puny. Sometimes they seem noble, sometimes contemptible.

As we read *Paradise Lost* we are often reminded of Macbeth and, as with Shakespeare's hero, we are often drawn in sympathy to Satan's side as he fights his doomed, ridiculous, magnificent battles with God. Both heroes arouse the same contradictory feelings about a destructive criminality which none the less compels some sort of admiration, and both arouse, very strongly, the same kind of pity. Macbeth looks at himself and his derelict life and decides that honour, love and friendship are things 'I must not look to have', while Satan looks at Eden or the unfallen Eve and, in the great soliloquies of his misery, thinks of everything he has lost and everything he has become:

> Ay me, they little know
> How dearly I abide that boast so vain,
> Under what torments inwardly I groan;
> While they adore me on the throne of hell,
> With diadem and sceptre high advanced
> The lower still I fall, only supreme
> In misery.
>
> > (*Paradise Lost*, IV 86–92)

The notes struck are very similar and the intense sympathy called up by each character is not to be denied. It tells us how far the living stories and characters take us from any simple judgement.

Milton is not, in Blake's words, 'of the Devil's party without knowing it', but he is notoriously restless with his myth, and the restlessness is creative. The author of *Macbeth* cannot be called restless, for the drama is of such limpidity that one cannot imagine a critic thinking its creator was of any party 'without knowing it'. But the complexities and tensions in *Macbeth* do none the less serve to draw the play away from its powerful status as an account of evil and destruction and towards the concerns of a different, later world, less Christian and less assured, where, in a different metaphysic, the doing of deeds is fascinatingly problematic. *Macbeth* has its Christian, traditional and even archaic side, but within its traditional frame and alongside its traditional content, there also lie other intuitions, modern and intractable, which give it life as a forward-looking rather than a backward-looking text. Alongside the radiant, Christian assurance and optimism of the play, there are endlessly dark, pessimistic intuitions of the criminal but heroic nature of all human doing or agency; and in the world of Romanticism, which this part of *Macbeth* foreshadows, fully foregrounded contemplation of the heroic criminal became one of the mainstays of tragic thought.

EXCURSUS 1: FROM *MACBETH* FORWARD – ROMANTIC SINNERS

A brief, introductory book like this should perhaps not digress too far into the difficult, speculative and slightly remote contexts of later art which contemplation of *Macbeth* none the less calls up to a modern reader; but a work of literature so immense in import cannot but stretch the mind that tries to comprehend it, so that forays and excursions beyond the boundaries of the play itself are sponsored by it, just as legitimately as close, exclusive scrutiny of its own details. Such forays into later art might set one thinking about Macbeth in relation to figures like Prometheus and Faust, by whose audacity as doers of deeds Romantic artists were repeatedly fascinated. They might set one thinking about him in relation to Melville's Captain Ahab, in *Moby-Dick*, whose black, destructive rage against a natural world he cannot subdue is as compelling as it is horrible and as daring as it is pointless. They might set one thinking about Coleridge's Ancient Mariner, as doomed by a single deed of murder as Macbeth, as criminally embroiled in violations of the inviolable, and as obscurely magnificent in his journey to the abysses of nowhere, where even the all-present God of Coleridge's Christianity is blasphemously absent.

In this later world, the greatest drama is not however to be found in Faust plays or Prometheus plays. The great drama of the world towards which *Macbeth's* modern subtexts draw us is the music drama. Even in comedy, such music drama, in the shape of Mozart's *Don Giovanni*, gave life to a figure whose compellingly unconditional energy, self-sponsored and unratifiable by any imaginable human morality, leagues him with the violators and extremists of what is normally a tragic vision; but for the greatest tragic exploration of audacious, criminal and wanton violation, committed at the extreme edge of the possible, we must turn to Wagner, to find, in *The Ring of the Nibelung*, primordial offences against the sacred quiet of the world which relate fascinatingly to the 'deed' of Macbeth that put 'a breach in nature'.

There are two breakers of the primal quiet in *The Ring*. The first is Wotan who, as the Norns narrate in the Prelude to the last of the cycle's four operas, *Götterdämmerung*, set going the long chain of fatal deeds and offences with which *The Ring* is concerned. In the quiet of the primeval earth he stood out as 'ein kühner Gott', 'a bold god', and in his temerity he was ready to pay the required price of mutilation of his physical–spiritual self in order to get the power for which he lusted. He was ready to sacrifice one of his eyes, savaging himself as he savaged nature by tearing a branch from the great ash tree and leaving the sources of life to wither.

The second bold disrupter is Alberich. In a kind of re-enactment of Wotan's original deed, further down the line of pollution in the dramatic present of *The Ring* rather than its narrated past, Alberich too acts boldly: 'Alberich zauderte nicht', 'Alberich did not hesitate'. He too is ready to pay in a different kind of self-mutilation, by forswearing love, and he too savages nature by tearing the gold from the rocks of the Rhine and plunging its waters into darkness.

They are both, like Macbeth, bold doers and interveners. They are immensely powerful in will, doggedly resourceful in pursuit of their aims, and capable of sustaining the resulting loneliness. Wotan may be the Alberich of light, 'Licht-Alberich', whose despotism is more or less benevolent and who believes in law, while Alberich is the Alberich of blackness, 'Schwarz-Alberich', who is utterly malevolent and who believes in slave-driving and humili-ation. There is an opposition between 'Schwarz' and 'Licht'; but both text and music stress the parallels and connections between the two as well as the combat, and thus concentrate attention on the similarities of all beings, of whatever kind and colour, who disrupt the quiet.

Wotan and Alberich, like Macbeth, tear something from the primeval fabric of things and cut into its wholeness. They seek power in separation of themselves from what Wagner wonderfully evokes in the music of the forest and the spring, the music of unpolluted water and streaming light, the music of the vast, effortless, radiant quiet which precedes the interventions of his two fatal Alberichs. In the beginning was not the Word. In the beginning was the forest, with the great ash tree in it, and the Rhine flowing through it lit with gold. These things were then desecrated and polluted by the doers, caused to wither and darken as the lonely quest for power began. *The Ring* follows the consequences of that quest down the weary but grandiose logic of its unfolding. It contains a great vision of light; and then it contains another, terrible vision of the light seized, and then bent and compacted into the fatal ring of gold while the rest of the world falls into darkness.

That Wotan's mutilation of himself involves the loss of

an eye is deeply symbolic, for the brightness of the eye
is central to *The Ring's* evocation of the radiant world of
light while the loss of the eye's brightness is a key image
of the world's darkening. *The Ring* is about the loss of
the light, and through it runs an imagery of eyes that
shine and then darken, linking verbally all the great light
passages in Wagner's music.

Wagner's sunlit world of bright rivers, forests and eyes
is akin to *Macbeth's* innocent world of the martlets, the
'delicate' air and the green boughs of Birnam wood. The
darkness into which it declines is akin to the murk and
perversion of *Macbeth's* 'fog and filthy air'. His profound,
sombre vision of how the human mind and will ineluctably
wound and pollute the world is in close congruence with
that part of *Macbeth* which probes the keywords of 'do'
'deed' and 'dare' in its exploration of the nature of
human agency. In both works the primal crime is the
interventionist deed of a great and reckless creature. In
The Ring that deed puts out all sorts of beautiful lights.
In *Macbeth* it palls things in 'the dunnest smoke of hell'.
In both works it is a matter of stabbing at the beautiful,
intricate pattern of things and making thereby 'a breach
in nature'.

In Wagner's operas, the primal crime is, as primal
crimes are apt to be, of irreversible consequence, for
Götterdämmerung, the last of the operas, does not sound
like a work in which the world is saved. *The Ring* is thus
sombre in the extreme, charting the irreversible logic of
pollution, the unavailing efforts of Wotan to devise a
means of recovery and the heart-breaking failure of
Siegfried in the impossible task of redeemer assigned to
him by the reckless god.

There is an equal sombreness in *Macbeth*, and an
equal, tragic weight in its exploration of the fatality of
deeds. It may end in the light, as *The Ring* does not;
but while its closing light is radiant and the redemption
it brings unforced and believable, our memory of the
play includes the dark, uncancelled. In so far as it does,

we derive from the play, or from a powerful subtext of it, something like the Wagnerian sense of an irremediable tragedy in the very fabric of things caused by the fact that deeds are endemic to the business of being alive and conscious, and yet at the same time are ruinous in their effects.

EXCURSUS 2: FROM *MACBETH* BACKWARDS – THE CHRISTIAN EPIC

But if *Macbeth's* subtext prefigures a later world in this way, its main text is still traditional and Christian. 'Romantic' element is there, but tracing it involves comparing foregrounded, visible themes from the later works with material from, so to say, the hinterlands and substrata of *Macbeth*. Macbeth is, like Wotan, the bold creature who commits the primal crime, but unlike Wotan he is also a treacherous 'butcher', ugly and black-hearted where Wotan is always capable of creating beauty and splendour, even in the midst of his ignominy and his reckless selfishness. To pursue such a comparison for too long would thus distort and glamorise a character who, back in Shakespeare's own world, tends much more to be regarded without glamour as a traitor and killer.

Shakespeare's world is, as ever, poised on the threshold between the medieval and the modern, and it is time, after this first excursus, to come back to the play's older, traditional side. In many ways this is one of the most conservative of Shakespeare's plays. Its sacred aspects, and particularly its sacred conception of kingship, give it an ancient, tribal quality, with long roots reaching far back into medieval tradition. We must examine these roots to restore the balance between ancient and modern which the play maintains.

Contrary to widespread belief, Shakespeare is normally sceptical about sacred kingship, and the naïve side of *Macbeth* which reveres it is a rarity, if not unique, in his work. In the history plays, Richard II and Henry VI are the two kings most apt to claim divine sanction, but it does them little good. The plays in which they appear are more worldly and less innocent than *Macbeth*. The real problematics of power are to the fore and no symbolic faith in sacred sanctions and taboos is enough to make anyone look or sound like a king, let alone make the kingdom work.

Richard aspires to be regarded as a sacred object, the 'anointed king', with his 'anointed body'; but while Duncan's subjects are sure that their king's body is 'the Lord's anointed temple', so that plunging a dagger into it is sacrilege as well as murder, Richard does not enjoy such unproblematic faith. He lives in a tough world of real politics where Bolingbroke, the secular, hard-headed usurper, is not so much a violator of the sacred as a potent, alternative image of what real power consists in, and the play looks calmly at him, biding its time as to what judgement might be made about the fascinating intrusion of the secular into sacred politics. In the unproblematic, naïve world of *Macbeth*, Duncan is never subjected to the mining doubts about the king's anointed body which are constantly present in *Richard II*.

Henry VI is a much finer and more profoundly religious man than the self-regarding Richard. He is gentle, innocent and pious, the 'holy Harry' of popular tradition, moved to tears by the sufferings of his subjects, while Richard is more taken by the sunset spectacle of his own misfortunes. But that, alas, does not underwrite holy Harry as king; indeed rather the opposite, for such otherworldliness makes him a liability as monarch, and peculiarly inept as a warrior-monarch in time of war. At his best he sounds almost like an early Hamlet, burdened with tormenting insights which more efficient men are spared, and through him Shake-

speare begins to explore the *Hamlet*-like intuition that
the real world is endemically inhospitable to men of
profoundly reflective consciousness.

But *Macbeth* is different. It alone is not concerned
with the problematics of real power. It alone defers to
the sacred–royal imagery and sets upon the stage a living
example of the divinity of kingship without subjecting
him to sceptical analysis. 'The royal play of *Macbeth*',
as H.N. Paul's study calls it, chooses to eschew Shakespeare's normal ironies about the anointed king. It
remakes the old fiction and gives unique life to its
traditional images. It asks no tormenting questions about
the pragmatic efficacy of such a king but uses him
instead as a symbol, an inalienable centre of solidarities
and loyalties so basic that no questions or problematics
arise. Murdering him is like striking at one of the
elements of life itself. It is like murdering sleep, chief
nourisher at life's feast.

No other Shakespearian king has this sort of status,
more like a Prince of God than a leader of men. *King
Lear*, as usual, shares something of this *Macbeth* quality;
but, again as usual, it mingles it with other things and
thus complicates what in *Macbeth* is simple. There is a
moment in *King Lear* when the loyal, traditionally-minded
Gloucester is horrified to think that Goneril will 'rash
boarish fangs' in Lear's 'anointed flesh'. It is a very
Macbeth-like image, with the same sense of sacrilegious
savagery as attaches to the 'gash'd stabs' in Duncan's
body. But even in *King Lear* the image of the king as
divine is far less fundamental than it is in *Macbeth*, and
plenty of problematic questions are asked about the highly
fallible individual who is by no means always given sacred
overtones.

Macbeth alone guards its naïvety, its visionary simplicity
and its radiant perception of a noble, heightened world,
utterly distinct from the blackness which Macbeth's crime
brings. One fumbles for words, but there is something of
what Nietzsche called the 'Apollonian' about it, with a

constant breath of the eternal in its images of nature, order and pleasure.

In this sense *Macbeth* is the least modern of all Shakespeare's political plays. Far from sending us forward to Wotan, Alberich, Prometheus, Faust or Giovanni, where a later world gave so much of its imagination to the solitary disrupter, it sends us back to an earlier art and an earlier world, where one of the literatures of the Christian Middle Ages regarded solitary disrupters as criminal deviants and gave its imagination almost exclusively to the settled world they betrayed. There is another, ancient side to *Macbeth* which relates closely to the primitive epic of the *chanson de gestes*, the 'song of deeds', that wonderfully naïve, epic literature of kingship and soldiering which knows nothing of problematics or irony and gives heart-whole commitment to bravery, loyalty, and Christian orthodoxy, all embodied in bright pictures of men who are the warriors of God and his King.

In many ways Duncan's nearest literary relative is the emperor Charlemagne from *The Song of Roland*, which was written down in twelfth-century France but dates from much earlier. The hieratic, venerable Charlemagne, white-bearded ('blanche ad la barbe') and hoary-headed ('tut flurit le chef'), is Duncan to the life. He is the symbol of all Christendom, and hence, as far as his poet is concerned, of all that is true, beautiful and humane. His warriors serve him, as Banquo and Macbeth serve Duncan in the early scenes of *Macbeth*, with unquestioning, high-hearted valour. Their world is without hesitation, their poetry without shadows. Bright, tapestry colours sing the deeds of a king and his small, mobile court of warriors. All are untroubled by doubt, as ready as the unpolluted Macbeth to 'unseam' a battle opponent 'from the nave to th' chaps' and guaranteed like him to be called 'valiant cousin' and 'worthy gentleman' for so doing.

In literature like this the verse gives its heart entirely to the collective, with their solidarity and loyalty in defence of Christianity and 'la douz France'. The poetry gives itself without doubt or irony to those who live loyally 'in the hand of the great God', and traitors to this world merit no regard at all. Ganelon, the poem's Macbeth-like criminal, is simply the black antitype to the fineness of Charlemagne's court. Little time is wasted exploring his possible motives, or the psychology of his treachery. He is just 'Ganelon, who committed treason', 'Guenelun, ki traisun ad faite'.

The part of *Macbeth* which is painted in the earlier scenes, when Duncan is alive, has this bedrock sense of loyalty to tribe, brought to life in the poetry of grace and decorum which surrounds the king, and in the unsophisticated, drums-and-trumpets magnanimity of the wounded Sergeant's epic verse. So has the play's ending, when simple, uncomplicatedly loyal men like the Siwards fight with the aid of 'the powers above'. To this part of the play the tragic hero is simply 'devilish Macbeth', and when his bleeding head is brought in against a background of green boughs we witness a scene similar to that at the end of *The Song of Roland*, where the blood of Ganelon is splashed on the green grass, 'sur l'erbe verte. . . espant', as the infamous renegade, the 'fel recreant', is torn to pieces by Charlemagne's horses.

This part of *Macbeth* is primitive, assured, and unshadowed. Its tenor could hardly be more remote from those elements in the play which, giving their exploratory, problematic regard to the great solitary rather than the group, send us forward to the lonely sinners of Romantic mythology. Not favourably inclined towards the mighty damned of Romantic tragedy and having no truck with the likes of Mozart's glamorous and brilliant nuisance, it brings the straying modernist to heel by celebrating the ordinary daylight with flawless conviction. This is the rugged, epic part of the play, stronger here than anywhere else in Shakespearian drama, and much stronger than anywhere else in the tragedies. It takes unqualified pleasure in the restoration of things to 'measure, time, and place'.

BACK TO *MACBETH*–ANCIENT AND MODERN

But the truly astonishing thing about *Macbeth* is that both parts of it exist and hang perfectly together, making many long centuries seem to turn on it as on a hinge. It embodies a vision of destruction on the Wagnerian scale and engages a sense of the fatality of deeds which need concede nothing to the great pessimists of the nineteenth century. It gives profound attention to the doomed, the destructive and the solitary, and with that attention goes an emotional regard which is fully aware of their status and greatness. It thus gives the world a hero such as Melville might have tracked to hell, Coleridge followed to the extremities of death in life, or Wagner pursued down the relentless logic of his and his world's undoing.

Yet at the same time it does not break faith with the Duncan simplicities, ending with the beautiful, unforced optimism of its daylight recovery. After all that blackness and blood, all that unstinted engagement with vain striving and doomed heroism, it finds at the end a nearly miraculous sense of liberation and renewal, created with an unemphatic elegance and lightness all its own.

Perhaps only Mozart's *Don Giovanni* has so capacious a double regard, both for the extraordinary solitary who flouts the world and for the more ordinary, flouted people who must live with him and endure his violating presence. *Don Giovanni* is in some ways like *Macbeth*'s comic twin, the supreme comedy of the night's disruptive mischief to match *Macbeth*'s tragedy of its horrors. The two works tell of a passage through the night, the one brilliantly comic for all that a tragic shadow stalks its story at every turn, the other a horrifying tragedy whose story none the less follows the festive–comic pattern of eventual release into the daylight; and the wonderful thing about them both is the apparent effortlessness with which they achieve this balance.

As far as *Macbeth* is concerned, this effortless balance

has everything to do with its double allegiance. It belongs equally to an ancient, secure, sacred world and to a modern, problematic one. Its wide embrace is thus given to something very much like the sombre pessimism of the Romantics; and then it turns back to its old, sacred traditions, lifted out of the dark by the Christian-sacred imagery of redemption and, even more, by a pagan-sacred vision of the woods' eternal re-greening.

· 3 ·

Men, Women and Babes

THE AGES OF MAN

A further characteristic which *Macbeth* turns out to share
with the medieval epic (and indeed to some extent with
Vergilian epic too) is its concentration on the masculine
world. In such a work as *The Song of Roland*, the small
court of warriors grouped about their king in defence of
the tribe presents an almost exclusively male image of
what matters most profoundly in the human world. In
the eyes of such a literature, women have no role to play
in the public realm where the central human values of
loyalty, solidarity and orthodoxy are created. It is men
who defend the frontiers of culture, playing a far bigger
role in the definition of the human than the women who,
left behind in 'la douz France', are stereotypically reduced
to a certain marginality with regard to the values which
epic embodies. *Macbeth* participates in these stereotypes.
It shares the epic conviction that, in public matters of
religion and tribe, what matters is male. Its imagery of
pollution is very largely female, its counter-imagery of
cleansing and recovery very largely male. Such things are
bound to make modern readers pause as they try to enter
into the play's imaginative world.

The women in *Macbeth* are allotted clear and limited
gender roles. Lady Macduff plays an entirely maternal

and domestic role, which she lives out in a beautiful, traditional portrait of madonna and child. On the other hand, it is a key part of the perversity of Lady Macbeth that she should refuse this allotted role. When she calls up spirits to 'unsex' her and take her milk for gall, and then vaunts her readiness to murder 'the babe that milks me', she is, in a way that the original auditors of the *chansons de gestes* would have understood, making an impudent, blasphemous attempt to divest herself of her female nature. Behind these images there is a strict and simple mapping of gender roles. In accordance with such a conception of gender, a woman has no business pushing herself into the public realm, no business trying to arbitrate as to what is and is not male by chiding her husband for his lack of masculinity, and no business seeking to outdo him in fearlessness and readiness for blood. In an imaginative world like this, such a woman can only be an abomination.

To this extent *Macbeth* raises some of the same awkward questions about gender as the earliest of Shakespeare's political dramas, where strong women, like Margaret of Anjou in the *Henry VI* plays and Tamora in *Titus Andronicus*, enter the male realm of power and politics with, in the eyes of the true-blooded men to whom that world properly belongs, something of Lady Macbeth's monstrousness. This is all very different from the comedies, where the world belongs largely to women and very few men are able to cut as fine a figure in it as the legendary line of great Shakespearian heroines, and very different from medieval romance too, which contrasts utterly with epic in giving the female world imaginative equality with, if not primacy over, the male. We take very easily to such works, but we may well have our imaginative battles to fight with epic and with *Macbeth*.

In its treatment of the witches, *Macbeth* again follows simple traditional rules as to the construction of the sexual order. The witches

                                should be women,
        And yet your beards forbid me to interpret
        That you are so.

                                        (I.iii. 45–7)

The horror of them is associated with the fact that they
are ambiguous, and that therefore, by defying clarity of
definition themselves, they flout and threaten all the
definitions and demarcations which constitute the order
of the cultural world. There can be no 'valued file' of
civilised categories, establishing roles and deciding on the
relative importance of things, if horrible ambiguities like
bearded (or unsexed) women are not strenuously opposed.
Such creatures pose the classic threats of religiously
abominable objects which offend against the orders of
'nature' and are thus to be regarded as deep sources of
pollution.

    Furthermore (and maybe causing still deeper trouble
for us) the task of cleansing the world of their polluting
influence requires not only males but peculiarly uncontaminated males. The young saviour, Malcolm, is not only a
man but a man 'yet/Unknown to woman'; the avenging
warrior, Macduff, is not only a man but a man not 'of
woman born'; and the young soldiers carrying the green
boughs of fertility will, in 'their first of manhood', take
part in an initiation which is not sexual but military, and
thus exclusively male. Such male avoidance of female
contacts is necessary to save the 'gentle weal' from the
havoc wrought by disruptive women. There are ancient,
primordial conceptions of the sexual orders of the sacred
underlying such things, and *Macbeth* would seem to tap
the potential of their characteristic images with continuous
assurance and without irony.

    Not all modern critics would agree with the notion that
these gender stereotypes are exploited 'without irony'.
There are plenty of modern readers who think Shakespeare
has presented the Duncan virtues as essentially limited if
not almost contemptible things, and a few for whom

the witches represent powers and freedoms rather than pollutions and horrors. Feminist critics have probed these aspects of the play in thought-provoking ways; but for those of us who cannot follow their lead in finding ironies which would make the play more hospitable to our scheme of things, the improbable power of its ancient imagery of gender presents an imaginative challenge of some complexity. One might have expected such a play to be rather alienating to later audiences, especially modern ones. It would certainly be very odd if a modern work were to set down imagistic foundations in such simple definitions of male and female, and even in the context of Shakespearian drama there is something exceptionally archaic about *Macbeth*.

It may be that this is an area of Shakespeare's drama and imagination destined to recede from us as our world moves on rapidly from his, but it looks for the moment as though we still respond to it well enough, making the necessary imaginative transfer to a remote world without undue strain. This is just as well, for the rewards of achieving imaginative access to *Macbeth*'s vision are unlike those furnished by any other Shakespearian play. The play's sacred vision of nature and mankind embodies a beautiful sense of the underlying cycles of life, and especially of such dualistic cycles as night and day, summer and winter, sleep and waking. There is something perpetually fresh and miraculous about the richness of such things. In another writer's hands they might have been wooden stereotypes, reducing life to an excess of pattern, but in Shakespeare's hands they feel as though they carry the innermost secrets of life itself which his play reaches down to tap.

These great dualisms are made to live in the mind by the vitality of the images which they sponsor. Against the visionary background of the cycles of life, the play draws a series of vivid pictures representing the major stages of human existence and setting out the pattern of life from birth to old age. There are babes in great number. Then

there are boys like Macduff's 'young fry' and Banquo's
Fleance; then Donalbain, the younger son of Duncan,
and ·Malcolm, the elder son, about to be named as his
father's heir. At such a moment a boy enters the world
of young men, passing on down the line as all the 'unrough
youths' of Malcolm's army do when they are blooded as
soldiers. From young soldiers we pass to seasoned
campaigners in the tribe's defence, like the wounded
Sergeant or the two 'generals', Banquo and Macbeth. Then
come older veterans like Siward, with sons of their own
coming to maturity, and the venerable Duncan himself,
an aged king concerned about naming his heir. Finally
the line comes down to such a character as the Old Man
of II.iv, a vatic figure who has completed the allotted
span of life depicted in the other images:

Threescore and ten I can remember well.

(II.iv. 1)

The hieratic, stately beauty of these images derives from
their calm. They are full of enviably unhurried acceptance
of natural processes, and of delight in the 'valued file' of
clear categories which a culture sets up on the basis of
mortal facts. They are almost all male, but their masculinity
does not feel imperious, exclusive or defensive.

Such pictures are all the finer, and what they represent
the more revered, because they depict this span of life not
only as a splendid but also as a fragile thing. The
allotted span should unfold in all its calm, satisfying
dignity, out it can so easily be broken, especially when
an irruptive doer of deeds like Macbeth is busy cutting
off lives at every stage. He kills creatures as young as
Macduff's 'fry' and as old as Duncan, the 'old man' in
whom Lady Macbeth is horrified to find 'so much blood'.
And in between he cuts off young sons, like Siward, who
'only lived but till he was a man', or mature parents like
Banquo and Lady Macduff. He even seeks to damage the
very roots of the whole system, or the seeds from which

the great lines of things grow, by getting at the 'germens' themselves and willing them to do his perverse bidding.

BABES

Perhaps the most distinctive visionary imagery in the play concerns the first stage of life in the cycle. *Macbeth* is the great play of babes. The first atrocities in the play are committed by Lady Macbeth when she summons infernal powers to 'unsex' her and boasts of her ability to dash out a baby's brains. The final atrocity is Macbeth's slaughter of Macduff's 'chickens'. We see on stage many young boys and 'unrough youths', together with apparitions of a Bloody Child and a Child Crowned; and we listen throughout to talk of children, babes, issue, breeding and nurture. The combined effect of the visual and verbal images can hardly be overestimated. *Macbeth* contains a veritable hymn to babes. Some of its deepest images of the goodness of life are found here, together with some of its most horrific images of the destruction of goodness.

In the earlier part of the play, Banquo figures as the breeding source of babes. He will 'get' kings, his 'children shall be kings', he will be 'root and father' to kings, 'father to a line of kings'; and his 'issue', beginning with Fleance, will run on in unbroken series to taunt unbearably the 'fruitless', 'barren', 'unlineal' Macbeth who must watch it all unfold with 'no son of mine succeeding'. Macbeth murders him for pragmatic reasons involving security and the succession; but there are also darker, more general motives, stemming from a barren rage against the creativity of things. This rage culminates in the witches' den when 'Banquo's issue' rises to torment Macbeth and all his impotent fury against them is felt in the exasperated pronoun 'his':

> Banquo smiles upon me,
> And points at them for his.
>
> (IV.i. 123–4)

In the latter part of the play, Macduff replaces Banquo in the central role of father to young children. When Macbeth turns to thoughts of 'his babes' at the end of the scene with the witches, his reasons are again not purely pragmatic. He seeks out those who 'trace [Macduff] in his line' not because anyone has prophesied that they will be kings but because the detestation of 'issue' now consumes him and the line of Banquo is beyond his frustrated reach. This renewed attack makes talk of babes proliferate again. We hear of Macduff's 'babes', 'your little ones', his tiny, impudently plucky 'egg', his 'young fry', his unguarded 'wife and child'. When he hears of their destruction his mind is overwhelmed by 'children. . . babes. . . pretty ones. . . pretty chickens. . .', and on the field of battle he is haunted by them: 'my. . . children's ghosts'.

Duncan is a father too, and so is Siward. There are 'Duncan's sons', and he, according to a lyrical and extravagant image from Macbeth which catches his envy of the circumstance, is:

> The spring, the head, the fountain of your blood.
>
> (II.iii. 96)

There is the singular 'son of Duncan' too, 'our eldest', named as heir by 'due of birth', the 'issue of a king' whose 'baby-brow' is crowned in the apparition of him, and Siward's 'right noble son', 'your noble son', 'your son' who lived 'but till he was a man'.

The play's male slant is felt in all this not only because it is full of sons rather than daughters (and fathers rather than mothers) but because the truly central image of babes and breeding sees them as born of men. Babes are issue born from seed. The innermost secrets of the procreative process are hidden in 'nature's germens' and 'the seeds of time', and nature teems and breeds from these germens. In a way which is exceptional in Shakespeare's work, the male-procreative imagery of issue and seed takes pride of place, not the female-procreative imagery of the womb. *Macbeth* does not contain the 'teeming womb of royal kings' of *Richard II*, nor the womb of nature which brings forth 'children of diverse kind' in *Romeo and Juliet*, nor the 'fertile and conceptious womb' of nature in *Timon of Athens*. It has none of the womb-fruit imagery associated with the pregnant mother of the Indian boy in *A Midsummer Night's Dream* whose womb is 'rich', with the pregnant Julia in *Measure for Measure* whose womb is 'plenteous', or with the pregnant Hermione in *The Winter's Tale* whose womb 'rounds apace'. The principal womb in *Macbeth* is that of Macduff's mother, which is not allowed to complete its procreative role before the Bloody Babe is 'untimely ripp'd' from it. The only other womb is that in which the exceedingly unmaternal Lady Macbeth is bade 'compose' the 'men-children' of Macbeth's dreams. These 'men-children', like the 'man-child' brought forth by the brutal, brassy Volumnia in *Coriolanus*, sound hard and armoured in comparison with the soft, vulnerable babes of Banquo, Macduff, and the rest.

But if for once Shakespeare sets aside his much used imagery of the fertile womb, he keeps the maternal role alive in his portrayal of Lady Macduff and reinforces the considerable visual impact of her scene with talk of the wren defending 'her young ones'. And he further keeps it alive with the imagery of milk and breasts which, unlike the womb, are not banished from his play's world. Lady Macbeth traduces her womanhood horrifically when she bids evil spirits come to her 'woman's breasts' and 'take [her] milk for gall', and she traduces all possible humane values when she thinks of having 'given suck' to the 'boneless gums' of 'the babe that milks me' and holds herself nevertheless capable of taking the nipple from it and killing it. Babes may spring from the male seed, but it is maternal milk which feeds them and maternal courage which, in one awful instance, tries to protect them from brutality. ⌊Maternal milk figures in such metaphors of gentleness and civilisation⌉ as 'the milk of human kindness' and 'the milk of concord',⌋ and may be thought of as nourishing the mighty, visionary babes of the play, 'heaven's cherubin' and 'pity, like a naked newborn babe'. It is also alive in people's thoughts of Scotland as their 'mother', or, in a word Shakespeare uses only here, their 'birthdom'; and it relates to the typically radiant imagery of nurture associated with the martlets, who 'breed' their young in a 'pendent bed' which then becomes the 'procreant cradle' of their infancy.

Such imagery restricts the female to a very fixed (maternal) role but is of extraordinary power none the less. And the power has to do with innocence, both the innocence of the life celebrated in the images and the innocence of vision which trusts them so unreflectively. An imaginative trust in the radiant power of innocence is one of the mainsprings of the play's vision, creating for example those sweeping pictures of the power of apparently vulnerable things like the newborn babe seen 'striding the blast' and the cherubim who ride horses across the sky, and this force which lies within innocence is an irksome thing to those who would be without it. The Macbeths are tormented to discover that they cannot kill it off in themselves. Macbeth feels humiliated by the fact that he is no more than 'the baby of a girl', Lady Macbeth finds herself disarmed and reverting to childhood in Duncan's room when she thinks he resembles her father as he sleeps, and Lady Macbeth again, immediately after this surprising visitation from the innocent depths of herself, talks scornfully of 'the eye of childhood' which hardened killers are better without.

Opposed to this powerful vision of procreation, birth and nurture as beautiful things at the core of life, there are images which dwell on vile forms of growth and breeding, or on violations of the breeding process. Such are the 'multiplying villainies' that 'swarm' on

Macdonwald, the 'birth-strangled babe' whose finger is one of the witches' ingredients, the 'nine farrow' eaten by their mother whose blood also goes into the cauldron, the 'new orphans' who cry every day under Macbeth's tyranny, the 'poor, innocent lamb' led to the slaughter to 'appease an angry god', the diverse troubles which deeds 'breed', and the griefs with which the world 'teems'.

But the greatest of the play's babes, introduced with grand, quasi-baroque rhetoric and saliently placed as key to the denouement, is Macduff himself, the apparitional Bloody Babe. There is a special grace in the fact that the great warrior-patriarch of the play is evoked not only as a father to babes but as a babe himself, and there is something magical and awesome about the way in which the violence and pain involved in his being 'from his mother's womb/Untimely ripp'd' is transformed into an image of victory. The *Macbeth* equation of strength with vulnerability animates the idea of a babe inauspiciously born becoming the dignified, mature and heroic Macduff. Before he is revealed he is heralded eight times as not 'born of woman' or 'of woman born', and the preparatory context of all the play's babes and birth-related images, added to these echoing phrases, makes his emergence as momentous as possible.

This is magnificent imagery, composing much of the play's deepest design. *Macbeth* is, amongst other things, a great, lyric poem dedicated to procreation, to the nurture of babes, to love and care for the very young, to the protection of them, and to the investment of hopes in them. Its deepest sense of the beauty and fragility of life-forms is found here, together with its paradoxical sense that what is fragile is also of immense strength. It may be that the secret of the play's radiant optimism, its sense of the light that survives the dark, is to be found here, rooted in the simple fact that babes are indeed innocent and vulnerable but also very strong. Nothing else in the play has quite the compelling visionary force of these tiny creatures, apparently defenceless but in the end overwhelmingly powerful. It is wonderful that a babe can stride the blast, that a bloody babe can overcome a tyrant, and that they both turn out to be stronger than anything that concentrated, ruthless will-power can muster.

It must surely be doubted whether our world's very different conceptions of gender really do set such things at a difficult remove from us, and whether we should respond to them with suspicion or with a search for irony. We certainly have to travel to reach *Macbeth*, as we have to travel to reach *The Song of Roland*, *The Aeneid*, or the epic and dynastic stories of The Old Testament, where great literature about the defence of culture and the establishment of value gives peculiar prominence to gender distinctions which are not only different from ours but precisely and awkwardly opposed to feelings which, at our moment in history, are of crucial importance to us. But literature is famous for its ability to travel and to inspire travel. It is famous for reaching across gulfs and for encouraging us to open our minds to fictions and imaginings which are not our own. And in the end it is famous for telling us that at some level they are in fact our own, being part of our present because they are part of our past, and the part of our past which can only be left in the past at the cost of our impoverishment.

· 4 ·

The Development of the Play's Action

THEATRE TIME

It is time now to turn to the play in scene-by-scene detail.
Dramatic works are not like paintings or sculptures. We
take them in over a period of time, piece by piece, and
we inevitably falsify how it feels to experience them when,
in memory, summary or critical generalisation, we conceive
of them as though they stood before us in a single, graphic
instant. It is fine, in memory, to balance an image from
Act I with another from Act V, rightly convinced as we
do so that a great poetic drama like *Macbeth* has complex,
internal coherence; but still 'the play's the thing', and the
play, in the book or in the theatre, comes in this order
not that, with these events not those. Theatre, like music,
is an art of time and timing, and criticism, adept in the
sort of embracing memory which collapses time, needs
always to come back to the sequential details of the literary
works which it is forever in the act of processing.

What follows is written rather briskly. It could have
been many times longer than it is, so rich is the texture
of *Macbeth*. It could also have deferred more to other
opinions, such as other critics have expressed or such as
I imagine readers might wish to put in counter-argument.
But I have gone quite quickly, not so as to be dogmatic

and impatient of the myriad other things which have been or could be said, but so as to have my say without too much insistence and then get out of the way to leave others to disagree as much as they want. There is no definitive version of *Macbeth*, no point in trying to write as though there were one, no point in literary critics getting bossy and bad-tempered about other people's views. I say my say, more by way of invitation than pronouncement, and leave the rest to other people's no doubt different ideas.

I look at the play an act at a time, starting each time with a description of how the act feels to me as an unfolding structure and then going into more detail about its individual scenes. *Macbeth* is as well paced and shapely as a great piece of music. I have tried to capture something of its different rhythms and the developing life of its five movements.

ACT I: INTO THE NIGHT

Act I of *Macbeth* moves from turbulence to serenity and back again. First come the witches, swirling through the 'fog and filthy air', and then the turbulence of the rebellion, where the 'multiplying villainies of nature' swarm on Macdonwald, a ragged band of 'kerns and gallow-glasses' swarm round him and 'the Norweyan lord' and 'the thane of Cawdor' are mentioned like unfamiliar heads bobbing in a crowd. Then comes a counter-movement, as the rebellion is defeated, the intruders scattered and the victors congratulated by their king. By I.iv we feel the emergence of a new settlement, with planting and growing, and by I.vi the swirling fogs have been dispersed and the martlets hang their nest in the clear summer air.

But this serenity is short-lived. The last part of the act brings a new kind of turbulence. Things stir ominously in Macbeth's unquiet, 'rapt' brain, and the act closes with

Lady Macbeth calling up 'thick night' and 'the dunnest smoke of Hell' and Macbeth's mind rocking and swaying to new hurly-burly rhythms:

> If it were done when 'tis done, then 'twere well
> It were done quickly. If th' assassination
> Could trammel up the consequence, and catch,
> With his surcease, success.
>
> (I.vii. 1–4)

The settlement was fragile and temporary. The play has plunged into still darker turbulences within minds possessed.

The play begins at a high pitch. Amidst thunder and lightning the three witches appear with no explanation as to who and where. Fragments of verse are shouted in the wind, words and forms whirl and disperse. There are rhythmic chants, brief shouts, and then they are gone again like rags in the wind. They have plunged us at once into the visual theatre of *Macbeth* and warned us of how fast it will go.

In I.ii the wounded Sergeant's epic rhetoric causes some critics to fret. But Shakespeare liked big, outdoor verse, and knew which characters to give it to. It suits the Sergeant, who is 'a good and hardy soldier' and a character in an epic play. The brave primary colours of his verse would not do everywhere. A soldier who spoke like this in *Hamlet* would not pass muster; but *Macbeth* is not *Hamlet*, Polonius is not present to complain that 'this is too long', and neither is the philosophical Prince with his intelligent but queasy views on dramatic decorum. Here the soldier's heroic idiom, continued by Ross in the speech about 'Bellona's bridegroom' and 'Norweyan banners' which 'flout the sky', strikes strong, clear notes, getting us quickly into the right mood for a play which sets store by the epic values they embody.

This idiom is not only brave and bright but also economical. Shakespeare uses it to paint verbal scenery, to run three separate historical campaigns from Holinshed together in seventy lines and to get his king on to the stage with his court, establishing its epic nature as intimate, mobile, embattled, generous and all-male. He also uses it to introduce two of the play's great images, for the Sergeant's 'gashes' prefigure those which Macbeth puts in Duncan's flesh, starting thereby the play's imagery of wounds and blood, and the 'surgeons' to whom he is delivered begin the play's arresting imagery of medicine and healing.

I.iii is one of the longest scenes in the play, but the rapid pace is sustained by its being broken into three short phases. For thirty-six lines the witches chant; for fifty-one lines they meet with Banquo and Macbeth; then the two generals, later joined by Ross and Angus, try to understand what has happened. There is thus no deviation from the *Macbeth* norm of rapid, short sequences.

Fierce speed is once more of the essence when the witches make their second appearance in this scene. The pace and percussive rhythm of them is frightening:

I'll do, I'll do, and I'll do.

(I.iii. 10)

There is something of the pounce of the Greek Eumenides in them, striking at people from afar to make them 'dwindle, peak, and pine'. The typical beat of their discourse is:

A drum, a drum!
Macbeth doth come.

(I.iii. 30–1)

One sometimes sees slow, brooding witches in the theatre, but attack, frenzy and disconcerting, sudden power are their true keynotes. 'They tingle in every fibre with evil energy', as Dowden says. Their rhythm is presto, their charm is 'wound up' very fast as they ready themselves for the kill.

They are also beings of immense import, not characters

from trivial superstition (such as Johnson amused himself with in a scornful, delightful, but quite irrelevant footnote-essay appended to their first appearance). They now call themselves 'the Weird Sisters', and are clearly fateful figures from legend whose powers are to be taken very seriously indeed.

Banquo, following them, begins wonderfully. He sees the witches' choppy fingers and strange beards. He sees that they are 'wither'd' and 'wild in their attire'. He says that they 'look not like th' inhabitants o' th' earth', and in that remark we hear for the first time something which, for want of anything better, we shall have simply to call 'the *Macbeth* sound'. We hear it again when, in his next speech, he talks of 'noble having' and 'royal hope', and ponders on things whose growth lies dormant in 'the seeds of time'. This *Macbeth* sound is gracious without formality, and its reverence is given to the inner processes of growth, the steady unfolding of time and the founding of human graces upon these breathing rhythms. We may not recognise it yet in Banquo's stray phrases, but we will when we have heard more.

This sound has, incomprehensibly to me, not always been heard in the play. The Arden editor wisely comments that:

> although there is no play in which evil is presented so forcibly, it may also be said that there is no play which puts so persuasively the contrasting good;

but this view, well-founded though I think it is, has not by any means been universally shared. Verdi, like most readers of *Macbeth* in the Romantic tradition, seems not to have heard the note which Banquo is the first to bring into the play. There is no '*Macbeth*' sound in his opera. No martlets are heard and a notorious piece of light-weight band music does service for Duncan's court, making Shakespeare's great and gracious Christian prince sound like the mayor of an Italian village. Legend gave the play to Macbeth, and even more to Lady Macbeth. Even now not everyone has an ear for Shakespeare's poetic evocation of this 'contrasting good'.

What makes Banquo summon up this beautiful sound, and think deeply about how proper 'inhabitants o' the earth' should look, is the witches' horrific strangeness. Above all it is those abominable male/female beards which defy the harmonious systems and categories of things according to the sacred orthodoxy of the play in which the good Banquo is a male believer.

These disruptive, supernatural abominations are devastatingly powerful. They are cunning too, observing the rites of high ceremonial with a triple salute to the iambic pentameter:

> *First Witch*   All hail, Macbeth! Hail to thee, Thane
> of Glamis!
> *Second Witch* All hail, Macbeth! Hail to thee, Thane
> of Cawdor!
> *Third Witch*   All hail, Macbeth, that shalt be king
> hereafter!
>
> (I.iii. 48–50)

followed by another salute, in the august monosyllables of the thrice repeated 'Hail!'. Then they simply *'vanish'*, unready to give up the preternatural rapidity of their habits at the behest of slow-witted humans, anxious to check chapter and verse, who beg such 'imperfect speakers' to 'stay' and explain themselves.

When Ross and Angus enter, the play begins to deploy one of its major imagistic resources. While the two new arrivals converse easily about high, royal things, the famous clothing imagery, which Caroline Spurgeon and Cleanth Brooks discuss in their studies of the play, begins to work. It is an uncomfortable Macbeth who asks them 'why do you dress me/In borrowed robes?' and perhaps a slightly absurd Macbeth too, reduced to dressing up as another man.

Banquo is holding on to his beliefs, remembering whatever instruction he may have received about 'instruments of darkness', but poor Macbeth is adrift already, plunging into the first of his extended self-communings. He tries to call up the sacred things which give structure and significance to the world, but the pellucid *Macbeth* sound, poignantly sought in talk of the 'seated heart' and the 'single state of man', is 'smother'd in surmise' and overtaken by 'horrible imaginings'. The structure of his world is being dismantled, with him fully conscious of the appalling process. Whatever it is that the witches have managed to implant within him begins to 'unfix' his hair and 'knock at' his ribs, with brute, physical force. The psychosomatic frame of the man is being pulled apart by 'supernatural soliciting' while his agitated silences separate him from his fellows.

Stalwart critics tell us at this point that it is Macbeth's fault, because he has free will and responsibility. (Milton tells us similar things about his many characters who give in to temptation.) But Shakespeare seems more guarded, and less punishingly sure about what culpability is. Even Banquo, a fine man and lucky enough not to be selected for ruination, shudders and reels before the witches' power. *Macbeth* is not a play in which incorruptible human stalwarts are ranged on one side and sinners on the other. There are no incorruptible stalwarts. Banquo, like the others, lives precariously exposed to what the witches are, and needs prayers, hope and luck to come off unharmed. Nobody is fully armoured against the witches; and if they were, this play would not respect them. Its respect is given to rather innocent people, uncorrupted by worldly suspiciousness, who can be duped as Macbeth is duped, or tragically led into such an error as Macduff makes when he leaves his family unguarded. Shakespeare will not allow us to think that Macbeth alone is made of fallible stuff. His scene ends with four 'inhabitants o' th' earth' going off together. Two of them are fortunate enough to have seen nothing. The third has

seen but has hung on. The fourth has been picked out,
and is already beginning to come apart. There is something
in his fate which smacks of the purest misfortune.

I.iv presents us with the small *chanson de gestes* court
again, where the settlement after the rebellion seems to
be going well. Even Cawdor, with the nobly insouciant
quality of his death, has a repentant role in it. But then
Macbeth enters with what ten thousand scripts, at O level
and higher, have noted as an instance of dramatic irony,
since here is another gentleman in whom the guileless
king has been building 'an absolute trust'. But irony, if
there is any, doesn't last long. The dominant note in the
king's greeting of his generals is much more beautiful than
dramatic irony:

> I have begun to plant thee, and will labour
> To make thee full of growing;
>
> (I.iv. 28–9)

and growing leads to 'harvest', as Banquo elegantly replies,
and must be watered too, in this case with tears of joy:

> My plenteous joys,
> Wanton in fulness, seek to hide themselves
> In drops of sorrow.
>
> (I.iv. 33–4)

Such speaking is elegant and courtly, but courtliness is
not normally as sap-filled as this. The *Macbeth* sound
thrives on living processes. It is also extremely emotional,
expressing strong, flowing, up-welling affections.

'Sons, kinsmen, thanes. . . ' is a more ordinary kind of
ceremonial sound; but there is a special magic even in this
kind of formal, fanfare simplicity as Duncan goes on to
make his courtiers sound like angels come to earth:

> signs of nobleness, like stars, shall shine
> On all deservers.
>
> (I.iv. 41–2)

Other Shakespearian plays contain high ceremony, but

none of it surpasses this. Its easy fluency seems never to be impeded by even the highest artifice. Such fluency, furthermore, is one of the play's basic indices of life, opposed by numerous images of blocking and stifling ('stop up th' access and passage', 'scarf up the tender eye', 'light thickens').

Macbeth does his best to join in, offering his own little fanfare in the form of the joyful welcome he and his wife will prepare. But he is again diverted, plunging inwards to 'black and deep desires'. He exits huddled in on himself, while the language of his fellows goes flowing on, rich with the pleasures of the social process and full of spontaneous largesse. His miserable separateness makes it very hard to think of him simply as evil. Could any of the others, had the witches chosen them, have resisted the vortex better than Macbeth?

There are three more scenes in Act I. In I.v we meet Lady Macbeth, with the witches' poison raging in her blood as if she had inhaled it from Macbeth's letter, and in I.vii we meet her again, stirring up her dilatory husband. In between come the martlets, so that the play's most sustained passage of serenity is placed between two examples of turbulence at fever pitch. I.v and I.vii are as awesome as anything in the drama of cruelty, madness and destruction. Nether Euripides nor Strindberg could overtop them. Yet in between there is a scene as fragrant as anything in the literature of pastoral lyricism. The suite of three scenes must rank as one of the greatest things in drama.

There is a sense of overhearing privacies and enormities when Lady Macbeth appears with the letter. The lid is off her repressions, and every worst impulse and half-thought pours wantonly out of her. The weighty verb 'to do' begins to beat its rhythms, and it sweeps her along to talk of pouring spirits into her husband's ear, just as his letter has poured them into hers. When the messenger brings news of the king's coming, her hectic speed increases and she announces the first of the play's thresholds:

>   the fatal entrance of Duncan
> Under my battlements.
>
> (I.v. 36–7)

She is, and will remain when Macbeth arrives, 'transported'. Her husband's arrival hardly interrupts her headlong excitement. He manages only fifteen words in the twenty lines he is on stage. 'Leave all the rest to me' is her unstoppable keynote as she drives along in a fury of 'business' and 'dispatch'. She prays for the perversion of everything that the *Macbeth* sound represents. She wants hoarseness not sweetness; she wants blood to be thick and passages to be stopped up, in imagistic opposition to the free flow of affection or tears; she wants the clear air to be filled with smoke and the blanket of the dark to smother the light. She has already identified milk with 'the milk of human kindness', and will thus pray for the destruction of human kindness when she wants her milk exchanged for gall. Her 'murdering ministers' and 'sightless substances' testify to her demonic fury, but also to the extraordinary and terrible energy which Shakespeare habitually perceives in nature. No writer's world is more dynamic, more swift-moving, more percussive, more dangerous than his, and no writer could therefore better convey the hideous foolhardiness of tampering with things of dreadful destructive potential.

She has her Shakespearian relatives, like Goneril and Regan in *King Lear* who share her cruelty and rapacity, Volumnia in *Coriolanus* who shares her driving will and Queen Margaret in the *Henry VI* plays who shares her impatience with a hesitating husband. She also has relatives elsewhere, for we can hear this note of furious, unleashed savagery in Aeschylus' Clytemnestra, Euripides' Medea and many of Strindberg's women. Why great (male) tragedians repeatedly give such moods to women is a question worth keeping open.

The martlets, by relieving contrast, delight in all that is 'procreant' and Duncan and Banquo delight with them.

L.C. Knights writes well about this scene, with its keynote of 'life delighting in life', as does Wilson Knight for whom it is one of the centres of *Macbeth*'s 'life themes'. It radiates light and fragrant air between two raging scenes of darkness. The *Macbeth* sound is played more sustainedly here than anywhere else, and henceforward we will always be able to recognise it.

Critical commentary can only fumble with the scene's opening ten lines where the poetic work is mainly done. The 'pleasant seat' has connotations of domestic content, but also of a general security and well-foundedness in nature at large; 'nimbly' reacts with 'sweetly', the sharp first word cutting the second to keep things tangy; the 'guest' speaks of hospitality and trust, and wonderfully dignifies the migrant birds as honoured visitors; the 'castle'/'seat'/'temple' makes all sorts of human building merge with the birds' nest in a harmony which dignifies both it and them. The 'loved mansionry' of these creatures makes for intimacy beween the organic bird and the inorganic stone, and the hard edges of the stone seem given the gift of life by their presence; 'heaven's breath' is clean and fragrant, to be smelled and, one would swear, to be heard like the breathing of a living organism; the 'pendent bed and procreant cradle' come from the very heart of the play's vision where everything to do with both sleep and child-bearing is constantly revered. But one might analyse it for ever and still not account for it. Where else can such a thing be heard? In Vergil? In Andrew Marvell? In the music of Schubert? Maybe in Shakespeare's last plays; but its real home is in *Macbeth*.

And then we are back to the night, indoors, listening to the dark introversion of a long soliloquy. We are back with doing, deeds and daring, and with the drives of mind and ambition. In the soliloquy that opens I.vii, Macbeth is helpless before the fascination of what he knows to be evil. The speech is one of the great examples of that unsleeping awareness of himself which makes him suffer every last torment of what he does, making Angelo his nearest Shakespearian relative and Milton's Satan his natural heir. He knows what it is to be 'meek' and 'clear', and such awareness makes self-loathing break in upon him like accusing angels of retribution, 'trumpet-tongu'd'.

These angels are part of one of the most extraordinary images in the play:

> his virtues
> Will plead like angels, trumpet-tongu'd, against
> The deep damnation of his taking-off;
> And pity, like a naked new-born babe,
> Striding the blast, or heaven's cherubin hors'd
> Upon the sightless couriers of the air,
> Shall blow the horrid deed in every eye,
> That tears shall drown the wind.
>
> (I.vii. 18–25)

Shakespeare thinks of a picture or map with babes puffing air and cherubs blowing trumpets to represent the winds, and out of that little commonplace his imagination conjures tempests of outrage that rise and rise again, with the foulness of Macbeth's deed blown by these winds like grit into vulnerable eyes. It sounds like a cry of protest against him, uttered by the entire world both natural and divine.

When his wife enters, there is a strong current of sexual combativeness of the kind for which Strindberg is the touchstone. She derides his lack of manliness and boasts of her own will-power in a display of extravagant, glamorous violence. Her performance brings him to submission, though not before he has made his noble statement about the proper limits of audacity:

> I dare do all that may become a man;
> Who dares do more is none.
>
> (I.vii. 46–7)

Johnson thought these two lines enough to secure Shakespeare's immortality had he written nothing else. They remind us of how fine a creature Macbeth is, or was; but that is not enough to save him now. The doomed couple are caught up now in a *folie à deux*, dreaming together of what they will do to 'th' unguarded Duncan' with the same sadistic relish which, in *King Lear*, moves Gloucester's attackers to savour and enjoy what they do to his unguarded eyes.

Macbeth still knows that it is a 'terrible feat'. He is neither hardened like Iago nor fortified with a sense of grievance like Edmund. He must do it gratuitously, which will require immense will-power and leave him with dreadful memories. We may safely surmise already that a man of his sentience will in the end be unmade by it. We do not yet know that about his wife, but we will before the next Act has finished.

ACT II: KILLING DUNCAN

Act II centres on the murder of Duncan. Its four scenes run to little more than three hundred lines, and everything is done to shape the whole act around the murder at its centre. It begins with Banquo and Fleance uneasy with foreboding and ends with Macduff, Ross and the Old Man looking back to the catastrophe. In between is the deed itself, done in the dead of night (II.ii), and its revelation in the first light of dawn (II.iii).

At the beginning and the end, unease is wonderfully conveyed. Banquo broods, worries, and starts suddenly when a figure looms out of the darkness, while at the end Macduff's lines are restive with subdued irony. In between, the darkness is full of terrors, shrieks and starts. Nerves are on edge and hairs on end. Bells and clocks sound in the silence, increasing jumpiness and deepening the silence when they stop. Torches stand out against the blackness. Macbeth's effort of will only precariously nerves him for the deed. Lady Macbeth has nerved herself with drink, but we still perceive the stresses and pressures which are now pulling her apart in her turn.

The act moves from profound darkness without moon

or stars to overcast daylight without the sun. There is a profoundly ambiguous dawn when the gate opens in the third scene. It brings light, but not much; and the revelation of the deed is also partial, since its true authorship is still obscured. Clothing is again important. When the morning callers enter and the crime is discovered, the stage fills with people in their night garments. The effect of sudden exposure and a household in disarray is powerful; and as they 'suffer in exposure', with their 'naked frailties' shivering unprotected, it is as if the deed had deprived them of all the panoply of their culture, leaving souls as well as bodies to shiver in the empty cold.

On this overcast night, lit by occasional torches, Banquo is wakeful. Shakespeare's realism knows that even the innocent are subject to 'cursed thoughts' when the restraints and guards of civilisation are down 'in repose'. The fearful dark brings out inner weaknesses and imperfections, even in the just. It also brings simpler anxieties, for when shapes come out of the night in a strange house where a king is lodged, old soldiers like Banquo stay edgy and alert: 'Give me my sword!'

When the torches reveal who is who, Banquo relaxes. He returns to talk of the King's 'unusual pleasure' and of the 'great largesse' which he has displayed to his subjects before retiring to sleep in 'measureless content'. Banquo has been dreaming, and the Weird Sisters are on his mind too, but he stirs back to saving life when Macbeth starts sounding him out conspiratorially. His 'bosom franchis'd' and 'allegiance clear' evoke the things he reveres, and for the second time in the play he reminds himself of them to save himself from the dark.

When Macbeth is left alone the phantom dagger appears, initiating his third major soliloquising plunge into the abyss. The dagger, appealing not to a 'bosom franchis'd' but to the 'heat-oppressed brain', and with sufficient force to 'marshall' him, embodies the hypnotic quality of the witches, and the nocturnal figure whom we see and hear on stage, talking to himself and clutching at the apparition as it draws him on, is again virtually helpless in the face of their assaults upon his mind.

In the latter part of the soliloquy, the poetry of nocturnal horror rises to a tremendous pitch. Bodies are tossed and tormented by 'wicked dreams' which 'abuse' sleepers, while curtains around beds, and curtains of sleep around the brain, cannot properly shelter people from the violent world outside. Howling, rapine and predation sound in relentless rhythm, and 'withered Murder' stalks the world like some allegorical grotesque brought to life by a fevered imagination. Macbeth is frightened of his own footsteps and terrified that the 'very stones' will speak out and expose him to an outraged world. The tolling bell at the end can sound at first like just such an announcement of exposure, until Macbeth gathers his scattered wits and declares it to be Duncan's death knell.

Writing like this testifies to Shakespeare's superb psychology; but it is also evidence of the emotional pitch and extravagance of his language and theatre. He could always write successfully at this near-melodramatic level. He seems to have been renowned for it on the Elizabethan stage, as is suggested by Robert Greene's envious abuse of him as the young upstart 'Shake-scene'; and within a generation of his death, when theatre had become a more genteel art, one of the chief tasks for the adaptation industry was to prune his wildness.

The terrifying pitch of this night-terror verse undergoes such correction in Davenant's version, which cleans up Shakespeare's primitive, nocturnal hocus-pocus to produce lines like:

Lennox   Good morrow, my Lord, have you observ'd
             How great a mist does now possess the air;
             It makes me doubt whether't be day or night.
Macduff   Rising this morning early, I went to look out of my
             Window, and I could scarce see farther than my breath:

The darkness of the night brought but few
objects
To our eyes, but too many to our ears.

Gentility and the Shakespearian theatre go very badly
together, gentility and *Macbeth* disastrously. As adaptations go, Verdi and Kurosawa are incomparably better
than Davenant, for the simple reason that they eschew
gentility and work at the relevant temperature. It is
incredible to us that Davenant's version supplanted
Shakespeare on the stage for seventy years.

There follows in II.ii even greater nocturnal horror.
The deed is done and the world's darkness seems absolute.
In the central part of the scene, where Macbeth gives
voice to his terror and Lady Macbeth says that such
thoughts 'will make us mad', two naked souls cower
together in an immense night. 'Shake-scene' is at work
again, with the tremendous inner drive and emotionality
of his native, theatre style.

First we have Lady Macbeth, speaking alone and
revealing the first chinks in her armour. Even with the
help of alcohol she has not been able to prevent a
compunctious visiting of nature, for Duncan 'resembled/
My father as he slept', and that memory of walking, in
her father's bedroom has a sudden beauty and innocence
in it. She was pathetically sure that such areas of feeling
no longer existed in her; but they do, and they tell us
that she too will not be proof against the ravages of
conscience and consciousness.

In the night's silence every last sound appals them. Such
a line as Lady Macbeth's:

I heard the owl scream and the crickets cry

(II.ii.15)

is extraordinarily charged, both with superstitious portent
and with pure, noises-in-the-night eeriness. Sound seems
to be greatly magnified, or imagined out of nothing, and

it is quite unclear where reality ends and fantasy begins. This theatre of the night's terrors has awesome theological significance as an embodiment of damnation, but it is equally an embodiment of simple fears, with the two protagonists reduced to children again by spookish noises. It comes to its climax when Macbeth thinks he hears a voice cry 'Sleep no more! . . .'. The imagined voice goes on and on like some protracted, unstoppable scream of protest issuing from the violated night and, as we have seen, crying out in its solitude like the owls, the crickets and the awakened sleepers. Animal, human and supernatural voices are not meaningfully to be distinguished. All are heard or overheard with the same weightless terror by the murderous children on the stage.

The Macbeths, for all that they cling together as one, still seem dreadfully alone, while some of the other human beings whose cries are heard do at least find a few shreds of companionship. To be 'two lodg'd together' in such a night is a wonderful comfort. To 'wake each other' and say prayers together constitutes a brief, spontaneous, creature contact such as Macbeth will never know again. Perhaps this lucky pair of sleepers are Malcolm and Donalbain; but even if they are the 'sleepy grooms', drugged by Lady Macbeth and later to be killed by her husband, they are still, in this one respect, fortunate men. The *Macbeth* sound can be heard in their prayers, as it can in the voice which, though it screams at Macbeth, also whispers to him, or makes him whisper, of the quiet, healing pleasures of sleep:

> the innocent sleep,
> Sleep that knits up the ravell'd sleeve of care,
> The death of each day's life, sore labour's bath,
> Balm of hurt minds, great nature's second course,
> Chief nourisher in life's feast.
>
> (II.ii.36–40)

Still Macbeth's helpless knowledge of what he is doing to himself goes remorselessly on. He knows 'twere best

not know myself'; but he does know himself, and with
tormenting clarity. That is why 'every noise appals' him
and why his bloody hands constitute a horrific sight which
seems to 'pluck out [his] eyes'. It is why just one of his
hands might pollute the huge, ever-moving ocean:

> this my hand will rather
> The multitudinous seas incarnadine,
> Making the green one red.

> (II.ii.61–3)

Macbeth's cry about his red hand is the very pinnacle of
horror at himself. It is impossible to exaggerate how
dreadful it must feel to perceive oneself to this overwhelming degree as the enemy of all nature and life. It is the
feeling expressed by Milton's Satan when he arrives at the
edge of paradise and

> horror and doubt distract
> His troubled thoughts, and from the bottom stir
> The hell within him.

> *(Paradise Lost,* IV 18–20)

In II.iii Macduff and Lennox call 'timely' to wake the
king, but before they appear we have the porter. Coleridge
thought his 'low soliloquy' had been 'written for the mob
by some other hand' and the Clarendon editors thought
it 'strangely out of place amidst the tragic horrors which
surround it'. Such views are rarer nowadays, but I confess
to sharing them. Something is clearly needed to give
Macbeth time to change his clothes for his next appearance
but the porter is arguably a ponderous device for solving
that simple problem.

There are two main difficulties. Firstly, Shakespearian
'low' comedy is normally livelier than the efforts of this
ploddingly obvious humorist; and secondly, the sacred,
heroic tenor of *Macbeth*, unique in the Shakespearian
canon, makes the play less hospitable to comedy than the
other tragedies. The porter's topical references to the
Gunpowder Plot help us to date *Macbeth* (or, more

strictly, his part of it), but otherwise all he really does is point a tediously overt moral about the gates of castles and the gates of Hell, intruding an alien element of black farce into a play which otherwise does not deal in it. He works well enough on stage so there is no need for me to grumble too much; but it isn't hard to remove him and make it work even better. The only thing he has in common with the rest of the play is that he too talks to himself.

When at last he shuffles off and the play returns to its normal idioms, a fine sense of early morning is conveyed by talk of 'stirring' and waking people 'timely'. We have seen how De Quincey and Verdi both felt this dawn to be symbolic as well as literal, but the symbolism is distinctly restrained so that real chill can be felt, together with a constant sense of the characters' stiffness and unease. Such awkwardness is well conveyed by Macduff and Macbeth's exchange about 'joyful trouble' and 'the labour we delight in', which sounds now gracious and now stilted. There is Macbeth's stiff control over himself and Lennox's puzzled speech about the 'unruly' night, and then Macduff's cry of 'horror, horror, horror!' explodes everything. From here to the end, the scene speeds on through panics, rough awakenings and sudden turns of suspicion before the agitated, half-dressed hosts and their horrified guests depart in confusion, leaving the stage to a curious little coda from Malcolm and Donalbain.

The major tonal contrasts of the scene are, as ever, simple and very powerful. At the beginning Lennox talks of 'strange screams of death', 'dire combustion and confus'd events' and the 'feverous' shakings of the diseased earth. At the end Macbeth talks about 'gash'd stabs', a 'breach in nature' and 'ruin's wasteful entrance'. Between these horrifying things there is the poetry of the *Macbeth* sound, coming sporadically in rich, stately phrases which celebrate 'the Lord's anointed temple', 'downy sleep', 'the wine of life' and the 'silver skin' of Duncan 'lac'd with his golden blood'.

Directors and actors must decide how Macbeth speaks his portion of these handsome lines. He may be dissembling, he may be clutching helplessly after things he has betrayed. The poetry will work in many different ways, but the contrast between the sacred and its destruction is its ever-present base. When Banquo thinks on the one hand of 'treasonous malice' and on the other of standing 'in the great hand of God', he sums up the polarities involved. He is remembering his beliefs again, and holding on to them while an entire world collapses.

Macbeth's slaughter of the grooms tells us much about the play. Killing men is horrible; but, in a way which testifies to the play's deep, epic sense of honour, it seems even more dreadful that he should try to kill their reputations. There is a dishonourable cheapness in such an attack on unsullied people. Trying to cut them out of the fellowship of trust seems almost worse than cutting off their lives.

But just as the scene starts with a problem, so it finishes with one, for the behaviour of Malcolm and Donalbain is much more curious than most critical accounts of the play suggest. It is surely strange that on hearing of their father's death they do not display grief, either when the others are still there or when they are alone, and stranger still that they never so much as mention the fact that he was their father. The absence of tears might be explained, for emotional paralyses of this kind do occur in states of shock. But they do not usually occur in Shakespeare's plays, where sons are normally moved to very strong emotions indeed when their fathers die. Furthermore, people in shock are not normally as cool as these two, and as full of wide-awake thoughts about their own safety.

Their behaviour would make them look a little shoddy in any context, but in the context of *Macbeth* it is particularly damaging. In epic, magnanimity is the rule, emotions are bold and even ordinary levels of expedient caution, let alone the astonishing cool of these two, are apt to sound niggardly. Epic men are not supposed to fret about their own skins, fail to find tears for murdered kings and parents, and 'shift away' so unbecomingly. There are many brave men in *Macbeth*, and many displays of strong, open affection. In such a world, it simply will not do to talk out of the side of the mouth about dangers lurking in augur-holes, or to need time to get your tears 'brew'd'. I frankly do not know why Shakespeare has drawn them like this.

Act II is rounded out by Ross, Macduff and the Old Man. On the one hand, 'dark night strangles the travelling lamp' and horrible appetites are evoked, in the case both of Duncan's horses, who 'ate each other' rabidly, and of 'thriftless ambition' which is said to 'raven up/Thine own life's means'. On the other hand, the Old Man talks of 'God's benison', Macduff evokes the 'sacred storehouse' of the royal tombs at Colmekill, and Ross remembers that those ferocious horses were once

Beauteous and swift, the minions of their race.

(II.iv.15)

The simple *Macbeth* contrasts between the beautiful and the vile still work strongly.

We have noted already how the brooding, half-averted manner of these speakers conveys perfectly their horror of the great sacrilege and the difficulty even of conceiving it. It also gives us our first experience of life under Macbeth's tyranny, where people do not dare to talk openly. Macduff already has his suspicions, the other two give little away as to what they may surmise. Shakespeare manages perfectly to convey how suspicion dawns quietly, how it hardly dares express itself, and how it divides people. Everything makes for a low-key, sombre ending to the act, full of omen and expectancy.

ACT III: KILLING BANQUO

Act III not only centres on the killing of Banquo but belongs to him throughout. It begins with his suspicions, leads on to his death and his son's escape and culminates with the appearance of his ghost. At the beginning he is hailed as Macbeth's 'chief guest' and acknowledged by the false king as having 'royalty of nature', 'dauntless temper', 'wisdom' and 'valour'; at the end he is remembered as 'the right valiant Banquo'. His stature throughout is magnificent, and to Macbeth nearly unendurable. Some critics have found him wanting, but I cannot understand why.

Macbeth seeks to make himself safe by eliminating this splendid figure, but in two respects Banquo refuses to die. On the psychological level, Macbeth cannot get out of his mind the slaughter of a noble man with whom he once shared *chanson de gestes* bondings of the most sacred kind; and on the plane of simple fact, Banquo's 'issue' eludes the hired assassins and from that issue will come King James, sitting perhaps in Shakespeare's courtly audience. The Act thus turns on the death and double resurrection of a figure whose invulnerability to death gives him a magical dimension.

Those however are long perspectives. Shorter perspectives present, from moment to moment as the play unfolds, scenes of violence and disruption so powerful as almost to banish all thoughts of recovery. But the underlying restorative rhythm is felt from time to time, and so is the helplessness of Macbeth, trying ever harder to impose his will on things but never quite able to do it. His force is such that he may swoop ferociously to the kill and put 'twenty trenched gashes' in Banquo's head. But then the ghost of his victim returns to cut him down to size and push him from his stool like the victim of a Puckish joke. He is thus huge and terrible, yet also, in other ways, pitiful and tiny.

III.i begins with Banquo's suspicions. Then music sounds and the new king and queen enter, with courtiers and attendants, talking of a 'great feast'. This is royal Macbeth and his feast is a grander affair than the one given for

Duncan at Inverness. That was private hospitality, this is a state occasion. Behaviour will be different, so will clothes, so will the palace setting. Each production must find its way of recording the threshold crossed, and the new station in Macbeth's life.

The ceremonial imagery of feasting looks and sounds well enough at first. It serves to evoke the grand idea of true kingship as well as the fact that Macbeth is only a sham king; and when the sham king thinks of the true one ('the gracious Duncan') and knows that he himself is a dwarf by comparison, the great images stand in stark contrast to his sad charade. This act, centred on palace and feast, records both the lost ideal and the new, corrupt reality.

In such a context, Banquo's 'royalty of nature' is a particularly awesome thing which makes Macbeth shrink pitifully:

> under him
> My Genius is rebuk'd, as it is said
> Mark Antony's was by Caesar.
>
> (III.i.54–6)

That sad confession makes him seem like a boy among men, and there is something childlike too in his puzzled rumination about the witches who 'put the name of king upon me'. All this humiliation is part of the punishing self-knowledge from which Macbeth's imagination never spares him. He knows what he has killed. He knows, in two awful images, that he has 'fil'd [his] mind' and put 'rancours in the vessel of [his] peace'. He knows he has thrown away the 'eternal jewel' of his soul, and that he has done it all pointlessly, so full of unstoppable growth are 'the seeds of Banquo' whose life he cannot kill.

He also finds himself hideous for having to resort to hired murderers, and no doubt for intruding them grotesquely into palace life. It is highly appropriate that he should look in horror at the company he is keeping and, confronted by these specimens, unburden himself of anguished thoughts about such 'shoughs, water-rugs, and demi-wolves' as make the intolerable claim that they too are 'men'. Macbeth's outrage at their claim is strangely moving. He knows how far the strengths of 'bounteous nature' proliferate diversely in all the breeds and species of the world's creatures, and some part of him still sets tremendous store by the orders and categories of the 'valued file'. With such perceptions still alive in him, he rounds upon the murderers with a desperation born of shame.

But his shame goes on, and the scene ends with all sorts of outrages. He tells petty lies, speaks coldly about how and where the murder should be done, and reaches a nadir when he tells the assassins to murder Banquo's child as well. Such things make him seem abject, adding a streak of Iago-like thuggery to the complex mix of his character.

III.ii brings more terrors for Macbeth and his wife and intensifies still further the language of the hero's torment. It contains two powerful images of the world which he destroys. There is firstly 'the frame of things' which, in a sudden burst of anger, he bids 'disjoint', and then the 'great bond' which, in more solemn conjuration, he bids the night 'cancel and tear to pieces'. The rage of both is terrible, as is the underlying imagery of torture which makes the disjointing and tearing to pieces horribly real. Yet still the drama makes us even more aware of his misery than of his evil. He is Shakespeare's most colossal criminal; but his mind is 'full of scorpions' and he is subject to 'sorriest fancies', 'terrible dreams' and 'restless ecstasy'. Such language makes us see misery rather than evil, moving us to profound compassion. However Christian Shakespeare may be, he is simply incapable of putting a Devil on the stage. He does not do it with Iago or Edmund, and did not do it with such early precursors of them as Richard Crookback, the murderous Clifford or the gloomy and violent Shylock. In each case his powers of empathy cannot help creating a human being with his own integrity as a character, resisting simple detestation or fixed categorisation.

Shakespeare's empathy takes us inside Lady Macbeth too, even though she is fast becoming a much less important character than her husband. When she confesses to living 'without content' and dwelling in 'doubtful joy', we hear traces of the Lady Macbeth whom Coleridge saw as a rather ordinary woman 'left much alone, and feeding herself with daydreams of ambition'. Within the apparent she-wolf there is a much more mundane woman, who sounds for a few moments like some kind of Emma Bovary, wanting her grim husband to show some style and be 'bright and jovial' at their dinner party. Such a note gives the heroic play a tiny trace of the sad humour of the Shakespearian banal. It is a note which we find everywhere in *Hamlet*, where Gertrude and Claudius are always trying to make Elsinore a cheerier sort of place where people are not so unaccountably hangdog. It is very restrained in *Macbeth*, but it does seem to be there, adding a shadow of the absurd to the predominantly heroic colour of things.

It is not long however before the heroic tone returns. When Macbeth says that the likes of Fleance are 'assailable', he echoes the dreadful tone of his wife when she noted how 'unguarded' Duncan was, and from here to the end of the scene everything is hideous. The bat, the 'shard-borne beetle' and the thickening light, which makes 'good things of day' droop and rouses 'night's black agents to their preys', are all grim, dreadful presences, while the image of the 'tender eye' stifled and 'scarf'd up' by the night, or sewn up as in the training of falcons, makes a peculiar assault on the nerves. By the end of the scene he has gone beyond any point to which she can follow. Even his appearance would seem to be different, for the 'rugged looks' which she would have him 'sleek o'er' seem to have borrowed some properties from the human 'shoughs' and 'water-rugs' with whom he consorted in the previous scene.

The murder of Banquo is swift, and the victim has no

great death speech. This is quick, ugly butchery such as
Iago would have appreciated. There are many eloquent
deaths in Shakespeare, from Romeo's to Cleopatra's, but
he is also the master of ineloquent death. His plays contain
banal deaths, deaths by sudden accident or quick design,
deaths like Hamlet's where there are no high words from
the hero to decorate, and thus perhaps mitigate, the banal
cruelty of extinction. Banquo's death is a miniature of
Hamlet's, giving us the same empty feelings about how
easy it is to put an end to a fine human consciousness
with a hired knife or a poisoned sword.

There follows the great feast scene. Critics and editors
regularly point out that banquets are symbols of order,
and that, accordingly, Macbeth begins this scene by talking
of 'degrees' while Lady Macbeth later registers its collapse
by telling the flustered guests to

> Stand not upon the order of your going,
> But go at once.
>
>   (III.iv.119–20)

This is true; but it is also true that the very stress upon
the ceremonial of order shows how false this version of
it is. Duncan was not such a stickler for hierarchies. His
was a court where a king could talk to an ordinary soldier
without fussing about order. There is room in this scene
to see the iconography and ceremonial of Tudor order,
but also to perceive the mock-Tudor as well. There is
again a whiff of Elsinorean, *arriviste* cheeriness in the new
royal couple's style of entertaining, which Verdi may have
been attempting to suggest when he gave Lady Macbeth,
rather bizarrely, a rousing drinking song. Lady Macbeth
has (I guess) been studying her books of etiquette and
learning their lore by rote:

>   the feast is sold
> That is not often vouch'd, while 'tis a-making,
> 'Tis given with welcome. To feed were best at home:

From thence the sauce to meat is ceremony;
Meeting were bare without it.

(III.iv.33–7)

These pronouncements are sometimes treated with great
solemnity by commentators, but the true beauty of the
Duncan virtues is never caught in them.

All this edgy social rectitude breaks down when Macbeth
hears that Fleance has escaped. The news sends him
floundering from terror to terror:

I had else been perfect,
Whole as the marble, founded as the rock,
As broad and general as the casing air,
But now I am cabin'd, cribb'd, confin'd, bound in
To saucy doubts and fears.

(III.iv.21–5)

Such 'casing air' is like a taunting recapitulation of the
Macbeth sound. The martlets used to fly in it. It was
miraculously able to give freedom and security at once,
holding breathing creatures in its embrace without squeez-
ing and oppressing them. Now Macbeth is shut in in
every possible way, in a cabin, in a crib, in a box, hardly
able to move or breathe at all.

But there is worse in store for him when the ghost
enters, more terrifying than 'the rugged Russian bear' or
'th' Hyrcan tiger'. The guilt and horror of his recoil from
it ('which of you have done this?', 'thou can'st not say I
did it') are wonderfully conveyed, and the silent ghost
itself, delivering its awesome messages without needing
words, is a fine creation. It is again the work of 'Shake-
scene', using the melodramatic traditions of the Elizabethan
stage to cogent psychological effect and keeping up the
high charge and emotional force of his theatre. Macbeth's
'genius' is, of course, even more 'rebuk'd' by the ghost's
presence than it was when Banquo was alive. It overwhelms
him with something of the same crushing power as the
witches wield.

But there is still room among these dreadful things on the heroic scale for some hints of the banality which makes us think of Elsinore. We get them when Lady Macbeth, embarrassed at the scene he is making, protests that this sort of behaviour simply will not do, and that it is typical of him to go in for such fancies. First a phantom dagger, now a ghost—what mayn't this impossible man think up next? For a moment we might seem to hear Emma Bovary again, chiding her feeble husband for his want of backbone, until talk of 'charnel-houses' and things 'too terrible for the ear' brings the high tragedy back to its normal tenor. It is of course psychologically very real that such daily oddments should get absurdly caught up in high, tragic events. Nobody knows that better than Shakespeare, even in this, the least 'mingled' of all of his tragic dramas.

Macbeth however is not thinking of daily things but of the beginning and of the end of all culture. He is thinking of how 'humane statute' first created 'the gentle weal' and fearing to see the world revert to barbarism again, with monuments becoming 'the maws of kites'. But even here there are some everyday presences. Macbeth was a brave warrior who would indeed have taken on a bear, a rhinoceros or a tiger, but there are realms where a tiger is less awesome than a mere 'summer's cloud' which can none the less 'overcome us'. When the brave Macbeth is 'overcome' in this commonplace way he draws our sympathy very strongly, for while it may be hard to relate to tiger-fighters, it is easy to be drawn to this more ordinary plummet of self-confidence.

We have noted the many asides and self-communings in this scene. The last of these, when he is alone with his wife, contains the play's most extreme example of the breakdown of discourse:

It will have blood; they say blood will have blood.
Stones have been known to move, and trees to speak;
Augurs and understood relations have

By maggot-pies and choughs and rooks brought forth
The secret'st man of blood.

(III.iv.122–6)

This is speech addressed to the air in utter distraction.
Words float through his mind without his having any
syntactical purchase on them. The opening 'it' hangs
suspended while he looks for a noun to attach to it.
Voices speak in his mind without his volition. Strange
correspondences between things are vaguely alleged to
constitute 'understood relations'. We grope in mists of
grammar, until the scene ends with the perplexed Macbeth
talking of 'my strange and self-abuse', which is a pitiful
summary of his condition and a further grammatical oddity.

No wonder he is desperate to find some fixed point of
certitude by returning to the witches. It is impossible to
live long in these hovering mists of doubt and dislocation.
Something must come to his aid; so he returns to the
witches as an adept, or addict, to be offered such
fortification as gives strength to a novice 'young in deed',
only however to be further sapped and undermined. Even
in his statements of resolution there is an underlying note
of hopelessness. There is the bold push forward and then
the confession that going on and turning back are both
equally 'tedious'. The logic of addiction in his dilemma
is clear and pitiful.

It is possible that Act III once ended at this point, for
Hecate in III.v is very probably spurious while Lennox
and the Lord in III.vi sound as though they belong in
Act IV, after Macduff has fled to England and while
Macbeth, hearing of it, 'prepares for some atttempt of
war'. There may, of course, have been something else
here to end the act; but it is also possible that a court
production, with devices enough to go in for a grand
transformation, might have passed straight from the table
of III.iv to the cauldron of IV.i. It would have made a
spectacular theatrical effect, with nicely eloquent moral
symbolism into the bargain. The two big, formal set pieces

run together would have composed a single, masque-like scene, constituting the centre of the play and containing two of its great visual displays. If this were once so, our Folio prompt-book text would relate to a production with more limited resources, where Lennox's scene was brought forward from somewhere in Act IV to leave time to get the cauldron ready.

However that may be, the Hecate scene does nobody any harm and III.vi makes a good ending for the act. Very few people will notice that Macbeth does not yet know about Macduff's flight, and if they do they are unlikely to mind. Lennox and the Lord, prowling warily round each other before daring to get to the point, show, for a second time, how tyranny creates mistrust and makes people afraid to use 'broad words'. The scene catches the awkwardness and indignity of roundabout talking too, with Lennox needing twenty lines to come out with the word 'tyrant' and twenty more before he dare mention 'our suffering country'. There is a touching realism in this, for the tapestry noblemen of *Macbeth*, lightly drawn as they in many ways are and not to be categorised as either heroes or cowards, react like people who, having had the good fortune to live in Duncan's Scotland, do not really understand what malevolence is. They would look less handsome in a drama of *Realpolitik* like *Coriolanus*, where we would find ourselves wanting them to buck themselves up, but they sound like fine and decent men in the naïve world of *Macbeth*.

They also contribute to the *Macbeth* sound. Lennox's praise of 'the gracious Duncan' and 'the right valiant Banquo' has the satisfying, secure feel of easily spoken, well-worn phrases, and the other Lord speaks beautifully about the social pleasures of the old world which Macbeth's feast could only mimic. When he hopes that

                              we may again
Give to our tables meat, sleep to our nights,
Free from our feasts and banquets bloody knives,
Do faithful homage and receive free honours,

                                          (III.vi.33–6)

we recognise the tone at once as the real thing. These pleasures sound like recollections of Eden. They create a strong sense of universal catastrophe and the postlapsarian cold. These are people used to living in clean, bright light. They are simply not equipped to breathe the 'fog and filthy air' into which their world has been dragged.

ACT IV: KILLING MACDUFF'S FAMILY

Act IV consists of two of the longest scenes in the play with a brief but powerful scene in between. The witches' den (i) begins the act with a celebrated set piece of visual theatre. The testing of Macduff by Malcolm (iii) ends it in an unusually subdued mode. In between there is the forced entry of Macbeth's *Gestapo* into Macduff's house (ii). Macbeth's status thus declines twice, first as he becomes an adept of the witches and then when he confirms himself as a hardened killer whose child-slaughtering assassins commit what both ordinary sensitivity and the other plays of Shakespeare persuade us is the ultimate cruelty.

But resistance to him is also confirmed. The whispers of suspicion and tentative suggestions of gathering counter-forces which closed the previous two acts are replaced here by clarity and assurance:

> Come, go we to the King. Our power is ready;
> Our lack is nothing but our leave. Macbeth
> Is ripe for shaking, and the pow'rs above
> Put on their instruments. Receive what cheer you may;
> The night is long that never finds the day.
>
> (IV.iii.236–40)

If two of the scenes are long, the characteristic quick rhythms of *Macbeth*'s action are still not lost. The witches' scene divides clearly into three parts, with the incantation and dance before Macbeth enters, then the apparitions, and then Macbeth's conversation with Lennox. Even the long, problematic third scene has its subdivisions. The

testing of Macduff constitutes its longest section, but there
are also two briefer passages, where the 'healing king's
benediction' is celebrated, and where Ross announces the
murder of Macduff's family.

The act contributes vividly to the theatre of symbol,
tableau and visual iconography. The cauldron, as we have
seen, is the opposite of the feasting table, but the witches'
coven is also to be contrasted with the play's civilised
settings and groupings, notably the court of Duncan. The
sexually abominable witches contrast with the domesticity
and femininity of Lady Macduff's scene, and her scene in
its turn relates back to the evocation of the martlets,
whose domestic nest is now matched by this human
nursery.

The witches' scene begins with animal cries. The mewing
of the 'brinded cat' and the whining of the 'hedge-pig'
break in with the same startling impact as the witches had
when they began the play by materialising out of the
murk. 'Thrice' and 'thrice' they cry, followed in manic
rhythm by Harpier's shrieking "'tis time, 'tis time!'. The
witches again wind up the pace of things very rapidly.
The rhythm and dissonance of the scene are fearful.

Wilson Knight's is perhaps the best description of the
incantation. In these random bits and scraps of the natural
world, torn from their true places and thrown pell-mell
into the cauldron, he sees the obscene opposite of the
play's beautiful 'life themes'. The cauldron is thus a
'holocaust of hideous ingredients', in which 'absurd bits
of life' bear witness to 'bodily desecration'. These eyes,
toes, tongues, legs and wings are ripped from their proper
places in the composed ordonnance of animal bodies, and
then human livers, noses, lips and fingers join them in
the odious brew. The chant is full of desecration and the
infliction of pain; and also of grotesque, parodic humour
whereby the 'meat' and 'sauce' of the royal banquet are
now malevolently caricatured to produce 'gruel thick and
slab'.

Nasty processes are involved in this cookery whose ingredients include exudings and secretions 'swelt'red' and 'sweaten' out of things. There is also something odious about the precision of the ingredients, for a long, well-savoured acquaintance with the dark lies behind such specialist requirements as the 'wool' of a bat or 'slips of yew . . . sliver'd in the moon's eclipse'. The witches are expert practitioners of a perverse pharmacy designed to harm rather than cure. Their poisons spring from the black side of Shakespeare's alchemical view of nature's powers, the menacing opposite of the medicines and curatives which lie secretly stored in plants.

It is characteristic of the witches, and of this black, primitive side of human experience, that they should fiddle with obscure racial fears by evoking the Turk, the Jew or the Tartar as stock phobias, and equally that they should know how to touch on dark taboos involving childbirth, abortion and infanticide.

When Macbeth enters he brings with him more ripping and ransacking in the shape of his readiness to see the whole 'gentle weal' plunge into ruin:

> Though castles topple on their warders' heads;
> Though palaces and pyramids do slope
> Their heads to their foundations; though the treasure
> Of nature's germens tumble all together,
> Even till destruction sicken—answer me.

> (IV.i.56–60)

This desire to ruin the procreative forces of nature at their point of origin represents the extremity of his attack upon life, but there is also awful bravery in his words. In the muscle of his verse and the temerariousness of his appalling desires there is still something obscurely heroic. At moments like this the Wagnerian dimension to his character becomes apparent. He is compelling like the 'bold god' Wotan, chilling like the rapacious Alberich, and riveting like both of them.

When the apparitions are called up, Macbeth sees the

dead Banquo for a second time, but this Banquo, though still 'blood-bolter'd', is not as awe-inspiring as the ghost who shook his 'gory locks' at him before. This Banquo 'smiles', and in so doing gives us the different key of this scene. What takes the stress is trickery, with terror as a secondary note, while earlier the balance of the two was the reverse. It is pitiful to hear Macbeth's ill-founded assurance that from now on he may 'sleep in spite of thunder' and 'live the lease of nature', and to catch in his phrases not some grandiose, dynastic ambition but a simple wish to sleep in peace and live out his life like everyone else, as he did before the witches ruined him.

But such moments of assurance are rare. For the most part his 'heart/Throbs to know', he is hungry to be 'satisfied', the witches 'grieve his heart' and their apparitions 'sear' his eyeballs. It is fearsome language, evoking the unremitting violation of body and soul. By the time the witches dance again and then vanish, Macbeth is a psychologically tattered creature, whose bold, Wagnerian audacity has collapsed.

He ends the scene by gathering himself again with murderous resolution. He is bent again on doing and deeds, but one of his images for describing these deeds also sounds the uttermost depths of pity. Duncan's sons are still infuriatingly alive. So is Banquo's son. The work of the germens is going on unimpeded, leading down that long, intolerable line of 'Banquo's issue'. The image which Macbeth finds to embody his hatred of it all contains an awful irony:

> From this moment
> The very firstlings of my heart shall be
> The firstlings of my hand.

> (IV.i.146–8)

Those 'firstlings' are the play's saddest babes.

The brief IV.ii can hardly help drawing forth the strongest response. Coleridge links it with other Shakespearian scenes involving children:

Shakespeare's fondness for children: his Arthur; the sweet scene in the *Winter's Tale* between Hermione and the [Mamillius]; nay, even Evans's examination of Mrs Page's schoolboy.

He finds the *Macbeth* scene itself 'dreadful', yet

still a relief because a variety, because domestic. Something in the domestic affections always soothing because associated with the only real pleasures of life.

His response to *Macbeth* is very strong. He recognises, from personal experience, the power of its presentation of 'delirious men that run away from the phantoms of their own brain' and 'the affliction of the terrible dreams', and the soothing relief of these 'domestic affections' is felt with corresponding intensity.

He is surely right to think of Shakespeare's children as a group. The intrusion of Leontes and his men into Mamillius' nursery in *The Winter's Tale* has some of the wantonness of this *Macbeth* scene, and 'his Arthur' is one of two examples from the history plays where Shakespeare goes out of his way to depict children as the pathetic victims of political violence, both he (in *King John*) and Rutland (in *2 Henry VI*) being portrayed as child victims of butchery even though in the chronicle sources they were young men of fighting age. In *Richard III* too, whose protagonist foreshadows Macbeth both as usurper and as victim of terrible dreams, Shakespeare is interested in the tyrant as the natural, predatory enemy of the very young.

The assault upon Macduff's family is perhaps the most moving of all Shakespeare's scenes involving child victims, partly because of its own intrinsic quality and partly because of its context in the play at large. The context of a male-dominated play whose other female presences are the unsexed Lady Macbeth and the bearded witches makes this mother and child in a domestic setting especially poignant. We hear new registers of the human voice in

the prattling of the 'poor monkey' and in the gentle
'natural touch' of Lady Macduff.

Into this domestic world come 'shag-ear'd' male adults,
related to 'shoughs', 'water-rugs' and other hirsute beasts,
but also equipped with daggers. Shakespeare hardly need
do more than put them on the stage to convey the sense
of intrusion and violation. There are therefore few words;
but some of those uttered by Macduff's young boy are
very important. Unlike Malcolm and Donalbain, Macduff's
son rallies quickly to the paternal cause. His defence of
his father's slandered name has something in common
with the moment in *King Lear* when Cornwall's servant,
unable to stand any more, rebels against his master's
savagery. In *King Lear*, that tiny incident involving a
minor character alters the direction of the whole play.
When Macduff's son tells the murderer point-blank 'thou
liest', a big shift of forces is likewise involved.

The last scene, nearly one hundred lines longer than
any other, has regularly made readers and directors worry.
The pace slows and the dramatic idiom changes. Such
modulations might work, and might indeed be welcome,
but they can make the scene feel somehow out of place.
I confess, in addition, to being one of those who has
trouble with Malcolm and his bizarre strategies. Such
laboriously extended caution as he evinces may well, as
the scene's defenders say, accurately represent what it is
like to live with a tyranny. But that point has already
been made, and within the play's normal idiom, by the
closing scenes of the two preceding acts. It is not clear
that such well-established themes need replaying, especially
in this curiously distant key.

The cautious Malcolm also runs into the problems
encountered when he and his brother fled after the murder,
taking 'our safest way'. He again seems soullessly worried
about 'mine own safeties' in ways that sound small-minded
in an epic context. The realist's 'modest wisdom' may
save him from 'over-credulous haste', but we may not
admire him much for it. 'Modest wisdom' does not stand

high in the roll-call of epic virtues. Homer's heroes would not have thought much of it and the medieval Roland would have scorned it as paltry stuff. They would all probably have regarded 'over-credulous haste' as the only man-sized option, and one suspects that Macduff might privately be of the same opinion. It is also unpleasant to see Macduff manipulated like this, and driven to come out with offers of whores and other 'foisons' for Malcolm to glut himself on. Strategies may be necessary sometimes, but tricking a good man into indignity by pretending to be a sewer is an oddly insensitive one.

Poor Malcolm will later have to play the difficult role of bringer of order and justice. Order-bringers, especially young ones unseasoned by experience, are often in danger of sounding a little slight. This may be used to ironic effect, as with Octavius Caesar at the end of *Antony and Cleopatra* who wins by no means all our sympathy as he takes over the world, and with Fortinbras at the end of *Hamlet* who, without a doubt in his head or the means to entertain one, wins still less. Malcolm however must later play the iconographic role of heaven-inspired saviour and as such he must be proof against irony. The poetry and dramatic iconography of the play's ending are so beautiful that he will in fact fulfil that role with all possible grace; but that achievement belongs to Act V, and it owes little to his unamiable performance in this earlier scene.

All this makes for awkwardness, but there are other things in the scene which work so well as again to stop the grumbling critic in his tracks. It both opens and closes with the time-honoured, imponderable dilemma as to whether the victims of political crimes should weep or resist. At the beginning of the scene they might 'hold fast the mortal sword' or simply 'seek out some desolate shade'; at the end they might 'dispute it like a man' or be able to do no more than 'feel it as a man'. Shakespeare's beautiful and succinct handling of such questions gave Verdi the inspiration he needed for his fine 'Patria oppressa' chorus and the aria 'Ah, la paterna mano' where

Macduff laments the failure of his paternal hand to defend his family. Between them they reproduce the two main Shakespearian concerns.

There are good things in the scene's central passage too, and marvellous things which survive as poetry and symbol even when the scene doesn't work well as drama. The sacred drama of pollution and lustration thrives on the hieratic, healing king of England, the equally hieratic Old Siward and the army of unblooded warriors who will cleanse the wounds of Scotland, bring magical healing as well as political liberation, and virtually bring fertility back to its soil. The image of the holy English king has a particular strength in this regard. When

> To the succeeding royalty he leaves
> The healing benediction,
>
> (IV.iii.155–6)

he recalls to mind both the line of 'succeeding royalty' carried before Duncan to Colmekill and the apparitional line of Banquo's issue leading down to the Jacobean present. The same idiom prevails when Ross brings news of 'signs and groans and shrieks that rent the air' and of men in Scotland dying 'before the flowers in their caps', where again the underlying symbolic life of the play's imagery leads it on towards its last phase.

At the end of the scene the general symbolism and the individual drama are once more unified in something of great power. When Macduff hears of his family's fate, it is overwhelmingly affecting as an individual human drama, while at the same time the general, impersonal rhythms go on, lifting the play out of the dark. Both personal grief and general recovery are respected, like two tunes played together. The scene ends with a ceremonial, symbolic sense of the emerging light:

> The night is long that never finds the day,
>
> (IV.iii.240)

while on the stage a private man pulls his hat upon his brows in an ordinary gesture of inconsolable heart-break.

ACT V: OUT OF THE NIGHT

The essential rhythm of Act V is not quite a function of its scene divisions. Editorial layout varies. The Penguin gives six scenes in all, the Folio seven, Alexander eight and the Arden nine, while the new Oxford caps them all with eleven. But the Act's true structure is that of a prelude followed by a three-phase denouement. The prelude is Lady Macbeth's sleepwalking scene. The first phase of the denouement alternates indoor and outdoor scenes as the liberating army advances on Macbeth's bunker-fortress. The second phase sees battle joined and sets soldiers from both camps on stage together in combat. The third phase depicts the outcome of the simple conquest when, after brief memorials for Young Siward, Malcolm delivers his great closing speech in celebration of the return to peace.

Several important structural features of the Act are perceptible as it unfolds. The central passage, alternating indoors with outdoors, is the most salient, but there are also many telling contrasts between the act's beginning and its end. It begins in the dark and ends in the light, begins with huddled, secret thoughts and ends with an atmosphere of trust, begins with lonely misery and ends with a joyous collective, and begins with a ruined life ebbing away and ends with youth and growth.

It must also be said that it begins with a polluted woman and ends with liberating men, among whom, as we have seen, Macduff and Malcolm have special credentials, uncontaminated by ordinary contacts with women either at birth or in sex. Verdi was probably unaware of the momentous change he made when he added a chorus of women at the end of his opera. They sing very tenderly, bringing thereby the opera's hymn of victory into tonal congruence with Shakespeare's beautifully non-triumphalist ending. But it is none the less the case that, merely by being women, they constitute a major, modern departure from Shakespeare's archaic original.

The sleepwalking prelude, in the depth of the night, set deep inside the castle and conjuring up Lady Macbeth's bedchamber hidden even deeper in it, is another of the play's great visual scenes. One may wonder whether the misery, injury and bewilderment of mental collapse has ever been so well figured in art. In one terminology this is a damned soul, in another a shattered psyche. Shakespeare's play embraces both terminologies. The distress of this figure, carrying her taper and then pitifully rubbing her hands together, could hardly be more moving, and the sight of her remains indelibly printed on the mind. A ghostly creature eaten away by what she has endured, Lady Macbeth might remind us of a figure from Kafka or Edvard Munch, the great modern artists of famine and malady. Verdi caught her well too, in the tragic and plaintive *'gran scena del somnambulismo'* which is one of the highlights of his opera.

Dress, as ever, is important. In the earlier dawn scene at Inverness, people were exposed in the 'naked frailties' of their night clothes and there was already something eloquently pitiable about them. Here, similarly dressed but now alone in her exposure, Lady Macbeth seems pitifully bereft of all protection. Lear braves the elements in similar vulnerability and near-naked exposure, but he is tougher than Lady Macbeth and much less irretrievably guilty. He is rescued, carried in a litter, laid in a bed, and clad in 'fresh garments' while medicines and music work to heal his injuries. But there can be no healing Lady Macbeth. 'This disease', says the doctor, 'is beyond my practice', and we do not expect to hear healing music in such a place as Dunsinane.

The doctors who wait upon exposed and mentally ravaged people in *King Lear* and *Macbeth* are very important Shakespearian characters. They are part of his vision of the world's alchemy. Cordelia treats the doctor in *King Lear* with deep respect and the doctor at Dunsinane, speaking tenderly of 'the benefit of sleep', 'infected minds' and hearts 'sorely charg'd', would seem to merit the same. Shakespeare's imagination is deeply stirred by healers and healing, and by the power of 'curatives' and 'simples'. He responds strongly to the magical-medicinal powers that reside, as Friar Lawrence puts it in *Romeo and Juliet*, in 'baleful weeds and precious-juiced flowers':

> O, mickle is the powerful grace that lies
> In plants, herbs, stones, and their true qualities.
> (Romeo and Juliet, II.iii.15–16)

This 'powerful grace' is the animating force within a dynamic natural world, alchemical, magical and full of curatives, which his verse conceives as a hive of interlinked, organic processes. Experts in such potent things, from Friar Lawrence through these two doctors to Prospero in *The Tempest*, are invested with immense significance. Herbalists, doctors and magicians are privileged custodians either of the womb of nature, where Friar Lawrence says 'children of diverse kinds' are bred in profusion, or of the *Macbeth* male variant where 'issue' springs from 'germens'.

The general context of the play increases the impact of Lady Macbeth's scene still further. The nourishing, healing tranquillity of sleep has been movingly evoked throughout, so when we see her wandering wakefully on the stage, or hear of her huddled in bed, with 'light by her continually', discharging her secrets into 'deaf pillows', the contrast is dreadful. Furthermore, this helpless patient was once a creature of terrifying self-possession who used to think that 'business' and 'dispatch' were her special province. Her 'great perturbation' and bewildered drifting are consequently redoubled in their impact.

The visual theatre of the scene has words to match. Its

verbal images of disease, mental torment and damnation are unforgettable, as is the contrasting language heard in the two watchers' talk of sleep and healing. The waiting Gentlewoman thinks of the disease from which Lady Macbeth suffers as a violation of 'the dignity of the whole body'. This body is psychic as well as somatic, and its dignity is no mere formal stiffness. Her phrase comes perhaps nearer than anything else in the play to summarising the meaning of the *Macbeth* sound.

After this dark prelude we move out into the air. There is still talk of malady, in the 'pester'd senses', 'the sickly weal' and a 'distemper'd cause', but what these men breathe is fresh air. This air is one of the great curatives which heals the cankered organism of Scotland. It comes with the green boughs and the soldiers' youth, with their easy companionship and the radiance of their language. A director must capture some sense of its cleanliness, freshness and spaciousness, and of the tight, unhealthy claustrophobia of the fortress. The young soldiers breathe 'the casing air' which in III.iv. was 'broad and general'. Macbeth, holed up in Dunsinane, is what was called in the same context 'cabin'd, cribb'd, confin'd'.

Such contrast between outdoors and indoors is a Shakespearian speciality. It is a major structural principle throughout the long sequence of his comedies where the forest of Arden, a wood near Athens, a wilderness near Mantua, a park in Navarre, a grand garden at Belmont, a lesser garden with a box-tree in Illyria and a 'pleached bower' and 'woodbine coverture' in Messina are repeatedly presented as sources of life, expansiveness and renewal, while houses, palaces, walls, corridors and public buildings are different, and usually more constricting. Something of the same contrast is used in *Hamlet*, where the thick walls of Elsinore shut out the fields and brooks where the mad Ophelia wanders; and the third act of *King Lear* creates an all-encompassing picture of wild nature and human society by alternating scenes on the heath with scenes in Gloucester's castle. The forest and the fortress at the end of *Macbeth* thus constitute a brief, brilliantly economical use of one of the most versatile of his motifs.

The soldiers in the open air speak with calm dignity, touching occasionally on the lyricism of the *Macbeth* sound. The besieged Macbeth by contrast rages, defies and bawls. The soldiers are together while he is alone. They carry 'leavy screens' while he buckles on armour. They speak the pellucid language of medicine and the 'sovereign flower' while he speaks of the 'sere' and the 'yellow leaf'. Their movement is of gathering, meeting and composing an order, while movement within Dunsinane is all chaos and ragged dispersal. Malcolm, a much greater figure now than he was in his earlier scenes, speaks his commands with a quiet voice, almost as if they were invitations:

> Let every soldier hew him down a bough
> And bear't before him;
>
> (V.iv.4–5)

while the desperate Macbeth is less polite to the wretched remnant of his followers:

> The devil damn thee black, thou cream-fac'd loon!
> Where got'st thou that goose look?
>
> (V.iii.11–12)

The young soldiers are carried along by the rhythms of time and by divine assistance which, even when 'industrious soldiership' is needed to 'advance the war', makes them seem hardly to be striving; but Macbeth has to steel himself to face their appalling presence, with an immense effort of will and much bluster.

Even his imagination now seems to be dying in him. It used to be the index of his human stature, and to expose him to endless torment. Now it has dwindled to the point where he has little response to the news of his wife's death:

She should have died hereafter;
There would have been a time for such a word.

(V.v.17–18)

His new, exhausted tenor is found in the soliloquies of despair, recording the 'petty pace from day to day' of a world evoked as shapeless, colourless, dimly lit and 'signifying nothing'. Self-referential on the dark stage of Dunsinane, he sees himself as 'a poor player,/That struts and frets'.

The nadir is reached when he resolves to die with 'harness' on his back. The 'giant's robes' he tried to wear always looked as though they were on a 'dwarfish thief', but even more humiliation is involved in his seeking to put on the trappings of an animal. The animal will fight, to be sure, and there is defiance in that. 'I will not be afraid' is a brave statement in any circumstances; but the keynote of this part of the play is despairing weariness. There are occasional flashes of anger, but not enough to stay the general dwindling.

In the second phase of the denouement, battle is joined and the stage is occupied by moving and clashing figures. Amidst the din we hear first the spontaneous nobility of Macduff which will not let him fight with

wretched kerns whose arms
Are hir'd to bear their staves;

(V.vii.17–18)

and then those beautiful, choric phrases spoken by Old Siward which capture all the lyrical ease of the triumph: 'the castle's gently rend'red', 'little is to do', 'enter, sir, the castle'. Macbeth is dwarfed by these two speakers. Macduff is an adult, seasoned, fine-conscienced man, and the venerable Siward an iconic figure, drawn with the usual *Macbeth* economy. Both are fathers to issue, men highly placed in the 'valued file' of things. The hunted, issueless tyrant is sad and dwarfish by comparison.

Siward and his son come straight from the history plays

where bonds of loyalty between father and son are always stressed. Their line reaches back to a seasoned soldier and his tyro son dying together on a battlefield in *1 Henry VI*. These are the Talbots, whose stalwart English heroism, celebrated in high-flown language and flamboyant gesture, contrasts magnificently (though chauvinistically) with the pettiness and dandyish refinement of Shakespeare's ever-caricatured French. It is brave stuff, by no means to be scorned; but in *Macbeth*, Shakespeare conveys as much in a handful of lines. It is an extremely economical double portrait of father and son, with the strong emotions that once stretched the glorious deaths of the Talbots over three Hollywoodian scenes still present within the austerity and chastity of *Macbeth*'s later style.

When Macbeth and Macduff are finally brought face to face, the contest is pitifully one-sided. Macbeth's sudden recognition of what the 'juggling fiends' have done to him has something in common with Othello's helpless awakening to the truth of Iago's machinations; and when Macduff reveals the nature of his birth and Macbeth finds at once that it 'hath cow'd my better part of man', we might be reminded of Coriolanus, reduced at the end of his play to a 'boy of tears'. Each of these three tragic warrior-heroes comes to a shattering, humiliating end, and Othello's description of himself as 'being wrought,/ Perplexed in the extreme' has relevance to all three. Their fates are of awful cruelty and the ends to which they are 'wrought' are as moving as any in tragedy. On the threshold of death, Othello has an extended scene of the utmost poignancy, Coriolanus has a briefer scene of complete bewilderment and Macbeth has simply the sudden shock of collapse and that oddly childlike cry of 'I'll not fight with thee'. There have always been critics proud to remain unmoved by one or other of them, in the conviction that they are getting no more than they deserve. It would be better if such critics left tragedy alone altogether, as of course they effectively have.

But Macbeth does fight, and against overwhelming

odds. With animal ferocity he confronts opponents who
are human, magical and divine. As with the harness on
his back, a reduction to subhuman status is involved; but
his defiant fighting also represents the last vestiges of his
tremendous nerve. As he faces such forces, the simple cry
of 'I will try the last' still has the power to impress us as
the product of a Wagnerian daring.

Shakespeare finds the perfect image for animality, as a
reduced yet compelling state, in the image of Macbeth as
'bear-like' and obliged to 'fight the course'. Even the great
Theseus in *A Midsummer Night's Dream* knew what it
was to fear a wild bear, and Macbeth himself had seen
the 'rugged Russian bear' as a worthy and formidable
opponent. The humiliated, captive version of this impress-
ive creature stirs the imagination in just the required way.
There is a long string of baited bears in Shakespeare's
plays, and they are by no means despicable animals. They
come 'roaring' in their chains in *Romeo and Juliet*, 'bay'd
about' by dogs in *Julius Caesar*, 'chain'd to the ragged
staff' in *2 Henry VI*, 'lugg'd' in *1 Henry IV*, tied 'by th'
neck' and 'head-lugg'd' in *King Lear* (as well as 'compelled'
in a possibly Shakespearian passage from *The Two Noble
Kinsmen*). He seems preoccupied by the humiliation of
such creatures, and by their admirable unreadiness quite
to submit to it, and there is no need to elect him to pre-
emptive membership of the RSPCA to perceive his
admiration for the animal's courage, or even for its simple
determination to roar and be damned. The company
Macbeth now keeps is still not quite without its doomed,
humiliated grandeur.

In the third phase of the denouement his roaring is all
done. The end of the play belongs first to Old Siward's
dead son, who 'has paid a soldier's debt', and then to
Malcolm and 'the grace of Grace'. One sometimes hears
complaints about Old Siward, as if he were an iron-
hearted stalwart, unready to weep tears for his dead son
and concerned only that he died bravely. This is to miss
the idiom of his part. An actor can put as much emotion

as he wants into his farewell to his son as 'God's soldier'; and it is in perfect key with the man, his role and the circumstances that whatever personal emotions he feels should be kept courageously down. The brevity of his utterances is part of the chastity of word and gesture which closes the play, and that chastity is imperative. We want no drums and trumpets, no fanfares and self-congratulations. The ending of the play is, and needs to be, subdued as well as festal. There are many different things to remember and many different emotions to feel about the action we have seen. Ceremonial must not try to drive out all these diverse impulses by insisting on a simple, triumphalist tone.

Verdi, the natural artist of Italian nationalism, gives his liberated *oppressi* a hymn of victory to sing. His ending contains lots of strong stuff about *la patria, il Re* and a retributive deity, addressed as *Dio vendicator*, who is as mindful as anyone else of the cause of the *Risorgimento*. It is hard to object to this, but the fact remains that Shakespeare is an altogether tougher tragic realist than his successor in the Italian romantic opera, and far too calmly bent upon awkward truths to wish, even in a Christian, royal and patriotic play like *Macbeth*, to send us away with our heads uniquely full of God, king and country. The great ceremonial of 'measure, time, and place' and 'the grace of Grace' is beautiful, and we come upon it with relief; but there are sombre memories to keep alive too, and a tragic sense, deeper and darker than any that Verdi ever touched even in greater operas than *Macbeth*, to which a subdued ending does better justice than a triumphant one.

Shakespeare is in fact the master of play endings which, like this one, combine the ceremonial of deliverance with a subdued sense of what has been witnessed and must not be forgotten. Even in the comedies, when everything comes out well and people find their marriage partners, he never indulges in an orgy of optimism. There are shadows, dissonances and darker memories to go with the wonderful, festive brightness. And when we come to the tragedies there can be no question of trying to efface sombre realities. None of the tragedies, not even the strongly ceremonial *Macbeth*, ever forgets that the living processes of tragic story, involving suffering, greatness and humiliation, should never be eclipsed in the mind, even by the most welcome kind of recovery such as closes this play with the birth of day after a fearful night.

· 5 ·

The Registers of Tragedy

MACBETH AND PITY

Trying to decide on the emotional tone of a Shakespearian tragedy is a hazardous, subjective business. Different people respond differently, each play lends itself to a great range of interpretations, and we are all capable of various reactions to any one play. In time we probably evolve a particular emotional register for each play, finding that *Hamlet* tends to move us this way and *Othello* that; but even this personal register is a changing thing, easily altered by a powerful performance. There can never be a common, agreed register, and there is no point in a critic trying to lay down the law about how things should feel.

I therefore offer some closing thoughts about the emotional impact of *Macbeth* in the certain knowledge that many people will not agree and that some will find my reactions inexplicably different from their own. Nothing can be done about that. T.S. Eliot was being excessively normative when he called literary criticism 'the common pursuit of true judgment', for our pursuits are not common but many and varied, and there is no such thing as 'true' judgement. But there is such a thing as the tolerant, liberal exchange of opinion (though Eliot was against it, thinking it a sign of atheism and decadence), and I offer my thoughts about the tonal register of

Macbeth as a contribution to that exchange.

I find what happens to Macbeth endlessly pitiful. I find him pitiful in his suffering, in his helplessness, and in that dreadful awareness of his own corruption which racks him incessantly and gives him 'terrible dreams that shake [him] nightly'. I find it pitiful that he envies, unendurably, men more fulfilled than himself, that he is duped with such facility by the witches, that he is ignominiously pushed from his stool by Banquo's ghost, that his stolen 'giant's clothes' are absurdly too big for him, and that he is a roaring, captive animal at the end. All tragic heroes are of course pitiful; but I find the pitiful element especially strong and continuous in Macbeth's case.

THE REGISTERS OF THE OTHER TRAGEDIES

It is of course obvious that Lear moves us to pity. He can be pitiful 'past speaking of', as a horrified and kindly observer puts it. What happens to him at the hands of Goneril and Regan, on the heath, and at the end when Cordelia dies, makes him pitiful in the extreme, as does the fact that he brings so much of it upon himself. But pity is still not quite the centre of what I feel. The man is such a colossus that astonishment and admiration take precedence even over the pity 'past speaking of' that his plight calls forth. His giant capacity to endure is, as Kent says at the end, a 'wonder'; and I find that a sense of wonder, at the greatness of his wrestlings with life, is nearer than pity to the play's centre of register.

Othello obviously moves us to pity, and so does Timon; but I find that the relentless, analytic realist in Shakespeare has put something peculiarly 'painful' (Bradley's reiterated word for *Othello*) into these two plays. There is something 'painful', and sometimes not far short of exasperating, about how these two heroes are great and small at the same time. They both have greatness of soul, are rich in ideals, and approach life with expansive generosity; but at the same time they are both so fallible, blind and self-involved that pity for them can sometimes have a hard time of it. They are in some ways pitiful just because of such things, but they are exasperating too, and occasionally almost incomprehensible as they fall victim to pressures which other people, greater or lesser than they, might so easily have withstood. It is extremely poignant and moving to see what happens to them, and how easily it happens; but something interferes with the kind of pure, unbaulked pity that Macbeth evokes, subjected as he is to pressures which nobody would feel confident of withstanding.

Timon makes one want to read lessons to him, as Apemantus does of course; and Othello can make one impatient to open his eyes. These are not comfortable feelings to have, for one does not wish to feel the slight element of critical detachment involved. But it cannot be helped. One can give all one's pity unchecked when Verdi lets his Otello die in unsullied nobility, seeing the appalling truth and recovering his romantic magnificence at once as the tremendous *bacio* ('kiss') music from Act I comes flooding back to him and all his love for Desdemona seems to flood back with it. A Verdi Timon would no doubt likewise have been allowed to go beautifully to his end. But the hard-headed Shakespeare is not minded to extend such unalloyed, pitying magnanimity to his Othello, whom he makes die with all his grandeurs and follies still intact; and Timon is left to compose his own self-dignifying verses about his 'everlasting mansion' while his author looks on in impassive silence. Right to the end of *Timon of Athens*, and to the overwhelming end of *Othello*, feelings of pity remain uncomfortably mixed with probing questions which we might wish to be without, and which the Romantic Verdi spares us.

Antony and Cleopatra live in yet another emotional register, which hardly has to do with pity at all. They make their choice of how to live, and then live out the

choice marvellously, if fatally. It may be a matter for
tragic sorrow that the world always makes their kind of
choice a fatal one, as it does for other heroic lovers like
Wagner's Tristan and Isolde and their medieval, romance
originals. It may be tragic, in other words, that life belongs
to Rome and that the Egypts of the world are never any
match for Rome's efficiency and power. But the truly
pitiful victim of that fact about the world is Enobarbus,
not Antony or Cleopatra. His death is heart-breaking,
whereas they, even in death, never lose their fire, their
magnificence, or, *faute de mieux*, their glamour, with
which they are enviably adept at loading every ignominy.
Their choice of life leads more to flawed magnificence and
fatal riches than to anything truly pitiful, and gives their
play a streak of carnival so strong as sometimes to make
one hesitate to call it a tragedy at all. We wonder at them,
admire them, are exhilarated by them and laugh both with
them and at them; but I think we pity them less than any
other tragic protagonists.

I begin to feel pity such as Macbeth evokes when I
watch Brutus, the true tragic hero of *Julius Caesar*. Brutus,
to put it simply, makes one feel sorry for him. His life
provokes continuous clemency of response, as we see how
a profound and honourable man, doing his disinterested
best to use his calm head and work out how to behave
in the common interest, brings about nothing but chaos
and carnage. What evokes pity is that he could hardly
have tried more, yet hardly have achieved worse, bringing
as he does ruin upon himself, his wife, his friends and
his country by trying to work out how a just and
honourable man ought to behave.

This brings Brutus tonally close to the two great
tragedies which have young people as their heroes.
Hamlet and Coriolanus are, like Brutus, remorselessly
overwhelmed by the worlds in which they live. The
penetratingly intelligent Hamlet and the brawny, unreflec-
tive Coriolanus have, for all their difference in brain-
power, much in common. Hamlet, the courtier-scholar

and 'glass of fashion', and Coriolanus, the heroic soldier of selfless bravery, are exemplary products of their worlds. Each is a young man who conspicuously embodies his world's ideals, aspirations and hopes. Each is therefore set up as a hero, and then exploited, preyed upon and driven to confusion.

At the end, each is assassinated. Hamlet is killed in the noble art of fencing by a cheat with a poisoned sword. Coriolanus is butchered by the henchmen of a rival warrior who cannot match his illustrious opponent by fair means and therefore resorts to foul. They have an idealism which makes them vulnerable and exposed in a world hostile to idealism, and their profoundly unidealised deaths, like the earlier scenes of their confusion and exploitation, are among the most pitiful things in Shakespearian tragedy.

THE OVERTHROW AND EXCLUSION OF MACBETH

The mature Macbeth is as defenceless as these two young men against the forces which decide to undo him, and his maturity only makes him the more pitiful. The brutality of what seizes him and flings him down is far beyond that of any force which the two younger men are asked to endure; and then he must also suffer ridicule and humiliation in his fall, as not only the victim of heroic catastrophe but also the clumsy dupe of trumpery. He is thus Shakespeare's supreme example of the tragic hero as a man utterly overthrown. While we may admire him for his greatness or detest him for his murderousness, I find that this rout of his being and his aspirations is the centre of his story. My last and deepest feeling about *Macbeth* always has something to do with having witnessed the dreadful dismemberment of a man's soul. The pity of it is the more profound since his dismemberment takes place against a background imagery evoking the wholeness and beauty of unviolated organisms with incomparable radiance.

In so far as some of these organisms are social rather than natural, the story of Macbeth's dismemberment is also the story of his banishment, and self-banishment, from the human commonwealth. This makes him the great excluded figure of Shakespearian tragedy. Other Shakespearian heroes are excluded in different ways, but none so completely, or from so much. Coriolanus is banished from Rome, Hamlet is excluded from what passes for normality in Elsinore, the black Othello suffers exclusion in white Venice and Lear becomes an archetype of man in isolation when the castle doors are bolted and barred against him. But the first three are lesser exclusions than that of Macbeth, who is banished virtually from nature itself, and even Lear's exclusion has its compensations. Some of what Lear loses is in many ways well lost, for the conception of human culture in the play is by no means uniformly flattering and to be thrust out from it is also to be set upon a great, creative quest. Furthermore, he is not alone, since other people accompany, follow, shelter and rescue him. Macbeth however, given the uniquely exalted nature of his play's portrayal of human culture, loses more than anyone else possibly could, and nobody seeks to join or rescue him. Nobody sees anything in him except what is to be abominated. His is the isolation of the damned. No other Shakespearian tragic hero endures it, and it makes him pitiful beyond all the others.

As an excluded man, Macbeth has his relatives in Shakespearian comedy, where there are more beautiful worlds than any that Hamlet or Coriolanus has to lose, and where some men find themselves excluded from all fellowship. Among these people, Shylock is the most developed as a tragic figure. Savage, gloomy, destroyed and self-destroyed, unfit for the lawns of Belmont, the polite society of Venetian Christians, and perhaps for finer worlds than theirs as well, Shylock is a great, early study of isolation which is genuinely tragic in tone. Then there is Jaques in *As You Like It*, a soured, darkly corrupted man whose self-exclusion from fellowship seems to stem from some obscure malady of the soul, Malvolio in *Twelfth Night*, 'most notoriously abus'd' by his laughing, easy-going neighbours for the stiff vanity which sets him at odds with them, and Parolles in *All's Well That Ends Well*, a hollow, unattractive creature, but pitiable none the less since he is humiliated beyond perhaps even his deserts.

Of these four lonely figures from the comedies, it is probably Jaques who most strikingly prefigures the plight which Macbeth suffers with full tragic force. Unable either to enjoy the forest or to return and enjoy the court, and with his soul diseased, according to the Duke, by 'embossed sores and headed evils', Jaques conveys a strong sense of a life which has begun to fall into Macbeth's 'sere'.

But if Macbeth's pitiful exclusion from fellowship has its roots in Shakespearian comedy, the violence involved in his overthrow is a purely tragic concept, and only tragic literature can provide true parallels for it. The play's conception of the savage powers that prey on human beings is as awesome as any conveyed by Greek tragedy where, far removed from the register of any comic drama, we find human beings brought to nothing by forces of irresistible magnitude.

The forces represented by Shakespeare's witches would have been recognised at once by all three of the great Greek tragedians. Their plays are rich in the sense of sudden catastrophe, and of wounding so cruelly directed as to seem born of malevolent will. They are strong in the sense of an extreme fragility in human lives lived under constant threat of ruin at the hands of savage, reckless or negligent gods. Their plays tell many stories of human beings overthrown, as Macbeth is, by irresistible forces inhabiting their own minds, because implanted there, at the slightest hint of an invitation, by gods whose bent for violence is hardly graspable.

In Aeschylus there are the Eumenides, who leap from afar to sink their claws into human quarry. In Sophocles there are such things as the sudden mania which possesses a helpless creature like Ajax, and a perpetual sense of the haplessness of human victims who, like Oedipus or Deianira, are enmeshed in things too powerful for any human being to withstand. And in the world of Euripides, most *Macbeth*-like of all, there is a barbarous, divine malice which seems to pride itself on what it can do to such puny individuals as it encounters in *Medea, Hecuba* or *The Bacchae*.

Central to Greek tragedy is a sense of the violence that falls from the skies, making havoc at will, reducing this or that life nearly randomly to ruin, and leaving behind stunned, pathetic or raging witnesses to its passing. *Macbeth* is in many ways the most Christian of Shakespeare's plays, standing out rather prominently as such in the works of an author whose mind in general shows no very special predilection for Christian terms and beliefs. But in its sense of the malice and violence which select people for pitiful overthrow, it is the most Greek of his plays, and perhaps the greatest recreation of a Greek tragic vision in all modern literature.

Bibliography

Bamber, Linda. *Comic Women, Tragic Men: A Study of Gender and Genre in Shakespeare* (1982)
Barber, C.L. *Shakespeare's Festive Comedy* (1959)
Bartholomeusz, Denis. *Macbeth and the Players* (1969)
Battacharya, Amal. *Four Essays on Tragedy* (1977)
Bayley, John. *Shakespeare and Tragedy* (1981)
Booth, Stephen. *King Lear, Macbeth, Indefinition and Tragedy* (1983)
Bradley, A.C. *Shakespearean Tragedy* (1904)
Brooks, Cleanth. *The Well-wrought Urn* (1942)
Brown, John Russell. *Shakespeare: The Tragedy of Macbeth* (1963)
  (ed.) *Focus on Macbeth* (1982)
Davidson, Clifford. *The Primrose Way* (1971)
Enright, D.J. *Shakespeare and the Students* (1970)
Erickson, Peter. *Patriarchal Structures in Shakespeare's Drama* (1985)
Evans, Bertrand. *Shakespeare's Tragic Practice* (1979)
Frye, Northrop. *A Natural Perspective* (1965)
Garber, Marjorie. *Dream in Shakespeare* (1974)
Grudin, Robert. *Shakespeare and Renaissance Contrariety* (1979)
Hawkes, Terence (ed.) *Twentieth-century Interpretations of Macbeth* (1976)
Heilman, R.B. (ed.) *Shakespeare: The Tragedies* (1979)
Honigmann, E.A.J. *Shakespeare: Seven Tragedies* (1980)
Howard-Hill, T.H. *Macbeth* (1971) (concordance)
Jorgens, Jack J. *Shakespeare on Film* (1977)

Kahn, Coppelia. *Man's Estate: Masculine Identity in Shakespeare* (1981)

Knight, G. Wilson. *The Wheel of Fire* (1930)
  The Imperial Theme (1931)

Knights, L.C. *Some Shakespearean Themes* (1959)

Kott, Jan. *Shakespeare Our Contemporary* (1964)

Leech, Clifford. *Tragedy* (1969)

McElroy, Bernard. *Shakespeare's Mature Tragedies* (1973)

Male, D.A. *Macbeth* (1984) (Shakespeare on Stage series)

Masefield, John. *A Macbeth Production* (1945)

Muir, Kenneth. *Shakespeare's Tragic Sequence* (1979)
  (ed.) *Shakespeare Survey* 19 (1966) (*Macbeth* issue)
  and Edwards, Philip (eds) *Aspects of Macbeth* (1977)

Nevo, Ruth. *Tragic Form in Shakespeare* (1977)

Oyama, Toshikazu. *The Tragic Cycle in Shakespeare's Macbeth* (1968)

Paul, H.N. *The Royal Play of Macbeth* (1950)

Ribner, Irving. *Patterns in Shakespearean Tragedy* (1960)

Rosen, William. *Shakespeare and the Craft of Tragedy* (1960)

Rosenberg, Marvin. *The Masks of Macbeth* (1978)

Sanders, Wilbur. *The Dramatist and the Received Idea* (1968)
  and Jacobson, H. *Shakespeare's Magnanimity* (1978)

Sen Gupta, S.C. *Aspects of Shakespearean Tragedy* (1976)

Spurgeon, Caroline. *Shakespeare's Imagery and What It Tells Us* (1935)

Tillyard, E.M.W. *Shakespeare's History Plays* (1944)

Turner, Frederick. *Shakespeare and the Nature of Time* (1971)

Wain, John (ed.) *Macbeth* (1968) (Casebook series)

Walker, Roy. *The Time is Free* (1950)

Watson, Robert, N. *Shakespeare and the Hazards of Ambition* (1984)

Williams, Gordon. *Macbeth* (1985) (Text and Performance series)

Index